Welcome to

THE

EVERYTHING®

PARENT'S GUIDES

AS A **PARENT,** you're swamped with conflicting advice and parenting techniques that tell you what is best for your child. THE EVERYTHING® PARENT'S GUIDES get right to the point about specific issues. They give you the most recent, up-to-date information on parenting trends, behavior issues, and health concerns— providing you with a detailed resource to help you ease your parenting anxieties.

THE EVERYTHING® PARENT'S GUIDES are an extension of the bestselling *Everything*® series in the parenting category. These family-friendly books are designed to be a one-stop guide for parents. If you want authoritative information on specific topics not fully covered in other books, THE EVERYTHING® PARENT'S GUIDES are the perfect resource to ensure that you raise a healthy, confident child.

Visit the entire Everything® series at everything.com

THE EVERYTHING PARENT'S GUIDE TO
Positive Discipline

Dear Reader,

When I was awarded my Ph.D. in counseling psychology and called my mother to let her know I was "officially" degreed, her response was, "Wonderful! Now you'll never have any more problems with your children." Not quite. Like any other parent, I mostly muddle through.

As for being a private-practice psychologist, that is actually a very humbling experience. Each day I learn more about how much I don't know. Thank goodness for my teachers. Every parent and every child and every family I have ever counseled with have each managed to teach me something about parenting I didn't know before. And I am forever in their debt for this continuing education. Much of my function as a psychologist is to pass this understanding along through counseling, giving public talks, and writing various books about parenting.

My purpose in writing this book is not to get you to agree with what I say. It is to get you to think about how you want to discipline your children. Please take what you like and leave the rest. And one final thing: *Enjoy your kids!*

Carl Pickhardt Ph.D.

THE
EVERYTHING
PARENT'S GUIDE TO

POSITIVE
DISCIPLINE

Professional advice
for raising a well-behaved child

Carl E. Pickhardt, Ph.D.

Adams Media
Avon, Massachusetts

Publishing Director: Gary M. Krebs

Managing Editor: Kate McBride

Copy Chief: Laura MacLaughlin

Acquisitions Editor: Bethany Brown

Development Editor: Karen Johnson Jacot

Production Editors: Khrysti Nazzaro

Jamie Wielgus

Production Director: Susan Beale

Production Manager: Michelle Roy Kelly

Series Designer: Daria Perreault

Cover Design: Paul Beatrice, Frank Rivera

Layout and Graphics: Colleen Cunningham

Rachael Eiben, Michelle Roy Kelly,

Daria Perreault, Erin Ring

An Everything® Series Book.
Everything® and everything.com® are registered trademarks of F+W Publications, Inc.

Published by Adams Media, an F+W Publications Company

57 Littlefield Street, Avon, MA 02322 U.S.A.

www.adamsmedia.com

ISBN: 1-58062-978-4

Printed in the United States of America.

J I H G F E D C B A

Library of Congress Cataloging-in-Publication Data

Pickhardt, Carl E.

The everything parent's guide to positive discipline /
Carl E. Pickhardt.

p.   cm.

ISBN 1-58062-978-4

1. Discipline of children. I. Title. II. Series: Everything series.

HQ770.4.P53 2003

649'.64–dc21

2003014701

Cover illustrations by Barry Littmann.

This book is available at quantity discounts for bulk purchases.
For information, call 1-800-872-5627.

All the examples and dialogues used in this book are fictional, and have been created by the author to illustrate disciplinary situations.

dis·ci·pline (dĭs′ə-plĭn) ▶ **n.**
1. Discipline is a combination of parental instruction and parental correction that teach a child to live according to family values and within family rules.

Acknowlegments

To Irene, with whom parenting has been, and continues to be,
an adventure, a delight, and a surprise.

• • •

Contents

CHAPTER 9: *Raising Responsible Children* . . . 95

CHAPTER 10: *Guidance: The First Factor* 113

CHAPTER 11: *Supervision: The Second Factor* 127

Introduction

PARENTING IS THE PROCESS of caretaking and education through which you help your child grow from a dependent infant into an independent young adult. Caretaking is a matter of expressing love. Education is a matter of training. As a healthy parent, you must provide both love and training to raise a healthy child. Providing love alone or training alone is not enough. Training without love can become extremely oppressive, and love without training can become overindulgent. In either case, a "spoiled" child can result—a child who is spoiled for healthy relationships later on because he is too socially compliant or socially domineering.

Discipline is part of a parent's training responsibility. Your job is to help your child learn "right" beliefs and follow "right" behaviors in life through example and direction. The definition of "right" depends on the traditions and values you carry into parenthood from your own personal experiences. No two families subscribe to exactly the same definitions of "right."

The Everything® Parent's Guide to Positive Discipline describes the different strategies for instilling discipline in your child in a positive way as he or she grows from infancy through adolescence. As your child changes with age, you must change your approaches to discipline to remain effective.

But starting out as a first-time parent can be a humbling experience. It is easy to feel overwhelmed by incompetence. "I'm responsible, but I don't know what to do!" "My child is crying, but I don't know what is wrong!" "I'm the adult, but I'm living on my child's schedule!" "I'm older and wiser, but my child is running the show!" The truth is, your children teach you how to parent as they grow. The truth is, parents are fast learners. The truth is, you know more than you think you do. The truth is, you will be able to figure out what you don't know at first.

Just to give you a headstart, however, here are six "A's" that most children want from their parents all through their growing up.

- Attention—listening and noticing
- Acceptance—understanding and interest
- Approval—valuing and praise
- Appreciation—acknowledgment and thanks
- Affection—love through telling and through touch
- Authority—rules and guidelines for living

Keep delivering these, and your parenting should be fine.

CHAPTER 1

The Basics of Discipline

C HILDREN ARE BORN totally dependent on external care and knowing nothing about social conduct. Your job as a parent is to provide stable support and nurturing love, and to create a structure of beliefs and behavior that your child can beneficially learn to live by. Your disciplinary responsibility is to clearly establish this structure.

Discipline is more than simply getting your child to behave the way you want him or her to or stopping your child from behaving the way you don't want on a specific occasion. Discipline is the ongoing process of positive instruction and negative correction through which your children are taught to act within family rules and according to family values. So, to state it simply:

DISCIPLINE = INSTRUCTION + CORRECTION

Positive versus Negative Discipline

To make this equation effective, you need to make one additional modification:

DISCIPLINE = 90% INSTRUCTION + 10% CORRECTION

Reverse that ratio, and the child's behavior usually gets worse, not better. Excessive negative responses from

parents tend to encourage more negative responses from the hurt and angry child. Angry parents who threaten, "And I will keep punishing you until your attitude improves!" only encourage a more sullen attitude in their child.

To discipline effectively, negative correction should be used sparingly, and positive instruction should be used most of the time. Animal trainers have used this principle for years to successfully train all kinds of wild and domestic creatures. They know that the only effective training relationships are those that hold positive value for the animal being trained. They don't punish failure or off-task behavior; instead, they encourage effort and success with rewards (known as positive reinforcement). It's the possibility of rewards that keeps the animal willing to work with the trainer.

 **FACT**

The most powerful way for parents to foster obedience is to reward every act of compliance by their child with appreciation, approval, or praise.

Athletic trainers also know to practice the positive. They know that for a champion athlete to remain a champion, she has to stay focused on what she's doing right. Certainly the athlete wants to know when she's doing something wrong, to try to fix it. But fixating on the negative is a great mistake. It encourages the person to ignore the vast majority of what is working well. Positive attention to what is going right keeps a consistent focus on what needs to be continued. Lose that positive attention and performance will begin to suffer immediately. The same principle applies when it comes to parents training their child in discipline.

How Discipline Affects Your Relationship

Consider the positive and negative responses that parents can give—rewards and punishments. Because children are pleasure seeking, they tend to repeat behaviors that are rewarded. Given a small symbolic reward like a stick-on star by his teacher for completing all his work today, the young child feels more inclined to complete his work tomorrow.

And because children are also pain-avoiding, they tend not to repeat behavior that is punished. Having to sit on the sidelines at recess and not get to play because she didn't complete her work, the young child feels more disinclined to neglect her work tomorrow.

Influence over Time

Initially, rewards and punishments seem equally influential because at the outset they often are. However, over time, repeated use of both methods reveals significant differences in the influence they have on a child. The more punitive a relationship becomes for a child, the less desire he has to cooperate with his parent. "Why should I want to do what you want if all you ever do is punish me?" The more rewarding a relationship becomes for a child, the more desire there is to cooperate with the parent. "I like doing what you want because you make obedience feel good."

 **ALERT!**

Positive or negative discipline treatment by parents affects how children learn to treat themselves. Children who are praised often are more likely to grow up to be self-affirming, confident adults, but heavily criticized children often grow into extremely self-critical adults.

Effective discipline relies on your relationship to your child. If you want your discipline to work well, then make sure you maintain a continually affirming relationship that he or she really values. Rely on instruction far more than correction, on rewards far more than punishments, and on being positive far more than being negative. Negative responses should be the exception, not the rule.

Changes over Time

In most cases, parents start off their parenthood relying primarily on the positive approach to discipline. However, as their son or daughter grows up through early childhood, then late childhood, and then into adolescence, a definite change in disciplinary approach often occurs. As their child grows older, parents tend to rely more on correction, use more punishment and fewer rewards, and generally become more negative than positive. Ironically, parents do this because they think this change will increase their influence. In fact, the opposite occurs. The relationship suffers, and they end up with less influence, not more. The less positive the relationship with parents becomes for a child, the less inclined that child is to do what the parents want him or her to do.

The 2-for-1 Rule

To keep this self-defeating transformation from occurring, there is a rule parents can remember—the rule of 2-for-1. For every negative response you make in your disciplinary role, make two other positive responses to the child within the next half hour. In this way, you communicate to your child that you see more positive value than negative value in him or her. It's not that you are backing off your correction. You are not. But you are working to limit any lasting injury to the relationship that correction, punishment, and negative communication can inflict, by re-establishing a positive experience once the misbehavior has been dealt with.

 **FACT**

Parents need to expect the obvious. Children will not always remember to follow rules they have been taught. Children will not always do what parents want. Through misunderstandings, mistakes, and misdeeds, good children will sometimes misbehave.

Instructional versus Correctional Responses

When your son or daughter has broken a rule or misbehaved, you must determine whether an instructional or corrective response is called for. If your child didn't understand the rule or value—didn't know any better—then you need to make an instructional response, explaining your position once again. "The reason for not saying I am away from home over the phone is that I don't want strangers knowing you are here alone for a little while. Simply tell the person that I cannot come to the phone right now, and ask for a number I can call back."

If your child did understand the rule or value—did know better—but chose to misbehave anyway, then a corrective response may be in order. For example, you may impose some negative consequence to discourage the child from repeating the infraction or behavior. This also demonstrates that you are serious about this particular disciplinary issue.

ESSENTIAL

Do not use correction with a child who didn't know what you wanted to have happen. "But you never told me!" cries the child, feeling betrayed by your unfair response. Hold your child accountable only for following rules and values that you've instructed her about repeatedly.

When you correct him, however, you should follow the correction with instruction (reteaching) so the child knows how to act differently the next time. Part of being reproached for doing wrong is being reminded of what constitutes doing right. "Because you knew that taking my tools without my permission is wrong, you need to help me clean up the house for an hour before going out to play. In the future, if you want to borrow something of mine, you need to ask me first."

Understanding Instruction

So how are rules and values to be taught? It can be hard sometimes to be a good teacher, but there are some guidelines that can help you approach instructional discipline in a way that will make it work.

Parents as Models

As the parents, you are the family leaders. Your actions do, in fact, speak louder than your words. If you keep complaining to your child about his or her complaining, you are sending a confusing message. If you leave your belongings scattered around the home for someone else to pick up but demand that your children pick up after themselves, you are sending a contradictory double message. Yelling at your children to stop yelling sends a self-defeating message. If you hit your children to stop them from hitting each other, you are sending a destructive message. In each case, you are modeling behavior you don't want your child to learn.

Setting Examples

More than what you say, giving your children an example to follow is important. If you want your children to learn patience, exhibit patience. If you want your children to listen to you, listen to them. If you want your children to control their tempers, then control your own. If you truly value patience, listening, and temper control, then promote your values with your actions. Be willing to model what you want your child to learn.

Bad Habits

But suppose you have a bad habit that you don't want your children to learn. Suppose, no matter how hard you try, you are usually late in keeping your appointments with family and friends, and now one of your children is starting a habit of keeping other people waiting. Is there no hope for helping your child to learn to be on time?

Yes, there is hope, because every parent gives two models for the children to learn from, not just one. Each parent models both how to be and how not to be. For example, you can probably think of ways you wanted to be similar to your parents and ways that you also wanted to be different. One of the things you may have liked about your parents was their self-sufficiency, and you have worked to be independent yourself. But one thing you didn't like was that they never asked you for assistance. As a child, this omission caused you to feel that you had no help worth offering. Not wanting to parent in the same way, you find yourself asking your children to assist you in ways you yourself were never asked. "My children know they have something they can contribute because I am always asking them for help."

Thus, when you see your child developing a bad habit you are struggling to break yourself of, you can offer yourself as a negative model. "This is a case of asking you to do what I say, not what I do. You know how I always keep everyone waiting and how irritating to other people that is? I think I do it because the closer I get to an appointment, the more I want to see if I can't get one more thing done before I go. So I end up being late and sometimes making other people who have waited for me late as well. I am trying to change this habit. I hope you can learn not to follow my bad example."

 **ESSENTIAL**

By honestly acknowledging your shortcomings and striving to correct them, you can use your mistakes to teach your children how not to be. But to do this, you must be able to let your children know that you are not perfect, giving them permission not to be perfect either.

Instructional Amnesia

Adults often forget how hard it was to learn the basics. An example of this instructional amnesia is the parent helping her young son memorize his home street address and phone number. The child seemed to know them yesterday but has forgotten them today. Irritated by the child's lapse in remembering information that is second nature to her, the mother explodes in frustration. "This is important! You aren't paying attention! What's the matter with you? You're not trying! Stop acting so stupid!"

The problem is not that her son isn't trying, it's that his mother has forgotten what it was like to first learn this kind of information many years ago. Knowledge has obliterated memory of ignorance.

Like most adults, once she knows something, it seems easy to learn. It is this instructional amnesia that causes her to be insensitive now, to become impatient, to express frustration by calling her child "stupid"—each of these behaviors making it more stressful for the child to learn. Instead, she should be using the difficulty her child has learning "something simple" to remind herself of how difficult childhood learning can be.

Remember what it was first like for you as an adult to learn how to use a computer? All the mistakes you made? How stupid you felt compared to your more technologically comfortable children? Well, that's how your child feels a lot of the time in comparison to you.

Learning by Repeating

Parents often believe children should learn something the first time it is taught, when this is usually not a realistic expectation. In most cases, children, like adults, are multiple trial learners. Not only do children often not learn something new at once, but having gotten it right before, they may get it wrong again. Learning really has two parts, not one. First, the child has to learn the skill or understanding, then the child has to learn to remember what he's learned. "I know the answer, I just forgot!" is a common and honest explanation.

Reminding and reteaching are part of the parent's instructional role. Also important is getting to know the kind of instructional approach that works best with your child. Notice which approach to following directions works best for your child. Some children learn directions best from being shown the steps or from seeing a description in written words. Some children learn directions best from being told and hearing it explained out loud. And some children learn directions best from hands-on activity, having some physical involvement to help them understand. Many elementary teachers use all three approaches to get information across. They put a homework assignment on the chalkboard for children to see, they read the assignment out loud for students to hear, and they ask students to write down the assignment in their notebooks to give students something to do.

 **FACT**

> Because it takes repetition to learn, it takes repetition to teach. It takes a child being willing to practice, the parent being willing to be persistent, and both of them being willing to be patient with however long learning takes. Impatience only impedes education.

Learning as a Risk

A parent's power of instruction depends a lot on sensitivity to the risks of learning their child must be willing to take in order to understand and master anything new. Consider five common risks.

- Your child must be willing to declare ignorance, to admit, "I do not know."
- Your child must be willing to make mistakes, to do things wrong before getting them right, to admit, "I messed up!"
- Your child must be willing to sometimes feel stupid, to have a hard time understanding, to admit, "I'm just not catching on!"
- Your child must be willing to look foolish, to have others witness his or her fumbling efforts to learn, to admit, "I must seem dumb to anyone who sees me struggle so."
- Your child must be willing to evaluate him- or herself or to be evaluated by others, to have his or her performance

judged, to admit, "My efforts show how well or how badly I can do."

You can choose to respond to these risks in a way that discourages effort, or you can work to reduce them and encourage your child to learn.

If you want to discourage learning, you can put down ignorance: "You should know this already!" You can act irritated with mistakes: "Stop messing up!" You can despair at slowness to catch on: "You'll never learn!" You can embarrass foolishness: "You should be ashamed at being so slow!" And you can give a critical evaluation: "You did it wrong again!"

 **ALERT!**

To keep your family environment safe for learning, don't let older children put down younger children's efforts to learn. Remain patient when your child makes mistakes. Treat problems not as sources of frustration, but as opportunities from which to learn.

However, if you want to support learning, you can give ignorance permission: "Learning begins with admitting that you don't know." You can treat mistakes as sources of instruction: "You will learn from your errors." You can be sensitive to feelings of stupidity: "It can be discouraging trying to learn something new." You can admire the willingness to look foolish: "You're brave to let others see you try." And you can give a positive evaluation: "You know more than you did before." Because learning is risky, parents must encourage their child to learn.

Giving Correction

You should not correct your child until you know for sure that he or she is old enough to understand what constitutes misbehavior.

This means the child is capable of learning rules, remembering them, and applying them to guide his or her own behavior.

Children under Age 3

Most children under the age of three cannot understand these rules yet. Patient, persistent, and positive instruction is the order of the day, showing preverbal children how to behave with playful demonstration, making it a game of imitation. Games of imitation are very powerful ways to teach a preverbal child who naturally wants to copy what his parents can do.

If your child grows tired and loses interest or resists what you want to teach, redirect her attention to something else. Bring the child back to the task at a later time to continue learning. The formula for much disciplinary training in early childhood is:

PLAY + PATIENCE + PRACTICE + POSITIVE ATTENTION =
PRODUCTIVE INSTRUCTION

When you need to correct your young child to discourage unwanted behavior (such as hitting) or unsafe behavior (throwing things), use the headshake "No." Gently clasp the child's hands, look him in the eye, and with a serious (not angry) expression, shake your head three times, and softly but clearly repeat the word "no." Wait a few seconds for understanding to sink in, then normalize the relationship by giving him a smile and a hug. When the child safely avoids doing what you have corrected, or has done what you wanted, be sure to reward that performance with approval and praise.

You must be especially sensitive when you correct your very young child. Expressing disapproval of actions you do not like before the child is old enough to know better only frightens and confuses the little boy or girl. For example, suppose your son spills a large glass of juice because he tried to lift it with just one hand, and now there is a mess to clean up when you were ready to relax. It's easy for you to feel angry because this event seems like something that could have been avoided. Once angered, you may be tempted to make a corrective response. What is really called for, however, is an instructional response: re-education. "Next time when you lift a glass so big, use two hands instead of one, like this. Now let's get two towels from the kitchen and you and I can clean up the spill." Afterward, thank him for helping to clean up. You may also want to practice carrying the glass with two hands so actions can reinforce his understanding.

Children over Age 3

With older children who have learned language skills, you can explain things because they now can understand from being specifically told. What you tell them must be specific and operational, not general and abstract. Tell your five-year-old to "clean up" her room, and you may get toys pushed out of sight under the bed, which is not what you meant by "clean up."

To say what you mean, specify the actions you want your son or daughter to take, give them one at a time, and sequence them until the whole job is done. "First, I want you to pick your toys up off the floor and put them in the toy chest." When this part of the task has been accomplished, reward it with your appreciation, and then move on to the next task in the sequence. "Now I want you to take the dirty clothes on your bed and put them in the laundry basket in the hall." If you don't give enough specific information about what you ask her to do, your child's performance will not match up with your intent.

 **ESSENTIAL**

Remember: Children will want to learn if their efforts are encouraged and rewarded, but they will be reluctant to learn if their efforts are criticized and punished.

If you have a willful child who has a hard time accepting "No," then choose not to say the word at all. Offer the child alternative choices instead. Rather than declare, "You can't use that tool," say,

"Here are some other tools I have that I can show you how to play with instead." You are teaching her that even when her first choice isn't allowed, other desirable choices are still available. What willful children want in particular, more than any specific object or activity, is the power of choice. So rather than just forbid what they want, offer them a number of other choices that are interesting to them and acceptable to you.

 **ESSENTIAL**

For very young children, positive responses, playful gaming, redirection, re-education, and an occasional use of the headshake "No" for correction should be all the discipline a parent needs to provide.

Principles of Correction

Correction should be reserved for known and deliberate misbehavior, and it should be given with care. Why? Because if given harshly, correction can threaten a young child's security and injure his self-esteem. Angry correction can cause your child to wonder, "For doing wrong in my parents' eyes, have I lost some of their love?"

The goal of correction is to get a positive behavior change from the child in a manner that creates as little negative impact as possible.

Consider seven principles of correction.

- **Reject the child's behavior, but never the child's person.** Don't say, "When you do bad, you're a bad girl!" When you tell her that her behavior is unacceptable, she still needs to know that she herself is as accepted by you as ever. A bad act does not mean a bad child. Children will be able to accept correction best when they know that misbehaving doesn't cause them to be loved any less. They shouldn't have to worry that they may lose your acceptance. "My parents didn't like what I did, but I know they still love me."

- **Don't give correction without direction.** Correction can be confusing and uninformative if all the parent tells the child is what *not* to do. The problem with negative commands—"Stop that!" or "Don't do that!"—is that they lack instructional power. The child thinks, "I know my parent wants me to quit complaining, but I haven't been told what I'm supposed to do instead." When you give correction, always include a constructive, instructional alternative. "I am more likely to listen to a cheerful request than an angry complaint."

- **Keep correction nonevaluative.** Correction is criticism enough. You don't have to add more negative content to an already negative situation by piling on statements of personal disapproval—"You should have known better, I've told you a thousand times! You've really let me down!" You've already told him how his action has offended your values or violated your rules. Therefore, simply say, "I disagree with the choice you have made, here is why, and this is what you will need to do in consequence to make up for what you did."

- **Stick to specifics.** Don't use abstract language to describe the offense: "You acted irresponsibly." "Irresponsibly" doesn't explain what it is that you're correcting. You must state the offense in behavioral terms so your child can understand and correct it. Describe the offense in specific terms as a happening or event. "You agreed to come straight home from school, but you stayed and hung around the playground for an hour instead. You broke our rule and you broke your word."

- **Keep correction educational.** How can correction of your child's misbehavior this time influence better behavior later on? The answer lies not in the severity of the correction, but in how well parents use wrongdoing to teach right conduct. Always fully discuss what was wrong with what occurred, what thinking and decisions led to this choice, and what the child is going to do differently so it does not happen again. For correction to have lasting effect, it must have reforming value.

- **Express appreciation for listening to and complying with the correction.** No child likes discussing what he or she has done wrong. No child likes enduring consequences for misbehavior. So to sit still for both negative experiences is hard for most children to do. If the child listened to you respectfully and worked off some consequence, that means he or she has cooperated with you, and you need to give positive recognition for that choice. "Thank you for hearing what I have to say, talking with me about it, and going along with what I wanted."

• **End by reasserting expectations of cooperation after correction is over.** Most of the time your child consents to act within the boundaries you define, getting along and going along with what you ask. Because infractions are the exception, you need to normalize expectations of your child after correction is done. So let her know that usual cooperation is anticipated. Always end correction on this reaffirming note: "I know you will do better the next time."

ALERT!

Keep your correctional response rational, not emotional. If you correct your daughter with anger, she may believe she is being corrected because you are angry, not because she did wrong. So she misses the instructional point.

The more frequently you choose to be corrective (and negative), the more you have to give positive responses between corrective episodes. If all you do is correct, then you have removed all positive incentives for cooperation. A child who believes "All I ever get is punished" has no rewards in the relationship for which to work. The more frequently negative you are, the more frequently positive you have to be.

CHAPTER 2

The Difficulty of Disciplining

I T CAN BE HARD FOR YOU to give your child the instructional part of discipline—it takes patience for you to give and practice for your child to accomplish. You may sometimes believe that it is easier to do something for the child than to teach her to do it right for herself. But this doesn't pay off in the long run. Disciplinary instruction is an investment in the future. Taking the time now to teach your child how to act responsibly does more than just give her a skill and a sense of competence—later on, her self-sufficiency will actually save *you* time.

And you may find the correctional part of discipline hard to provide, too, because neither you nor the child welcomes this negative focus in the relationship. As a parent, however, you know that every wrong your child commits is an opportunity to teach your child what is right. Thus, although you wish your child had not drawn on the bathroom mirror with your lipstick, you could use that opportunity to teach her about the privacy of your belongings, why it was inappropriate to color on the mirror, and how people must clean up when they make a mess.

Your Attitude Matters

Parents need to be on guard when repeated discipline problems occur—on guard against themselves. When a child does something wrong, parents can also respond in the wrong way. Discipline problems can change a parent's outlook and behavior in ways that make the situation worse and not better. Your fatigue, frustration, or anger can adversely affect your view and treatment of the child.

A discipline problem can cause parents to:

- Develop a negative perception of the child: "He was born to make trouble." (No child is born to make trouble.)
- Make generalizations about the child instead of sticking to specifics: "She has no respect for what I say!" (The child was simply arguing about not being allowed to have a snack before supper.)
- Narrow their perception of the child: "All he ever does is wrong!" (The parent ignores all the child does right.)
- Take personally what is not meant to be personal: "Why is she tormenting me this way when I'm so tired?" (The child is too self-occupied to consider the effect of her arguing on others.)
- Feel helpless and hopeless: "We've tried everything and nothing works!" (No parents have ever tried every management alternative; they have only grown tired and run out of the will to try anything else.)

 **ESSENTIAL**

If you become so fixated on the problem that your view of the child becomes negative, get support. Ask a friend to help you list ten things that are going right in your child's life and ten qualities in your child that you value. This can help restore your perspective.

Guidance for the Future

A child is in many ways an adult in training. Who and how a boy or girl learns to be in childhood and adolescence are much of who and how he or she will be as an adult. The best predictor of how your child will behave in the future is how he behaves now. Therefore, to affect your child's future, you must be active in the discipline he or she is learning now.

Avoiding Bad Habits

If she has been lying to escape responsibility, she is likely to resort to lying to escape responsibility in the future, unless you address this issue with discipline. If he has been bullying people to get his way, he is likely to resort to bullying to get his way in the future, unless you address this issue with discipline. These are bad habits you don't want your child to develop. How the child learns to behave determines much of how the adult will act. Through the discipline they provide, through the behaviors and beliefs they encourage their child to practice, parents are literally shaping their child's future habits.

ALERT!

When your child gets into a bad habit like whining, don't try to break it with punishment. Instead, don't give in to whining, but encourage a replacement habit: "Practice asking me cheerfully, and you may have a better chance of getting what you want."

Promoting Good Habits

Since discipline is a matter of teaching habits, be thoughtful and intentional about the habits you want your child to practice now that he or she can rely on later. For example, ask yourself what habits related to spiritual faith, character, integrity, nutrition, exercise, work, relaxation, play, personal organization, hygiene, health, communication, treating people, responsibility, or service to others you want to teach. Then decide what specific activities you can encourage the child to do to help him develop these habits.

For example, to develop a sense of integrity, you may choose to encourage your child to act in accord with his or her values. To teach him to communicate well, you may encourage your son to speak up and be honest. To make sure she practices good nutrition, you may encourage your daughter to eat a balanced diet and limit how much junk food she eats. To build good work habits, you may encourage your child to earn the things he wants and to finish what he starts.

If you are not modeling the habits that you would like your child to learn (for example, if you're demanding timely work from the child when you often procrastinate yourself), then try to change your conduct to show the child that with effort and practice habits can be changed.

Risking Resentment

Discipline is the hard part of parenting. The rewards are not easy to come by, and parents often feel they are investing a lot of energy for what often seems like limited gains.

In the process, you often risk your good standing with your child. He or she resents you for your efforts, and you'll likely hear phrases like:

> "Oh, why do I have to do this!"
> "Oh, why can't I do that?"
> "You never let me do anything!"
> "You always make me do what I don't like!"
> "I don't want to talk about that now!"
> "Why can't you just leave me alone?"

Children of any age are unlikely to say to parents, "Thanks for the discipline."

Not a Popularity Contest

Because providing discipline is often an unpopular part of parenting, parents who crave popularity with their children may find it hard to do. Parents may feel insecure when they displease their child, feel guilty when they cause unhappiness in their child's life, or try to avoid conflict at all costs. This causes them to shy away from setting a requirement or making a refusal. Or, under the pressure of the child's displeasure, they will relent on what they declared the child could not do. What looks like a problem of a willful child is often a problem of parents with insufficient courage and resolve to say no.

 **FACT**

A child who learns not to accept his parents' refusal as an answer soon dominates parents who can't stick to saying no. Without being able to rely on firm parental authority, the child is at risk of getting in trouble as a result of getting his or her impulsive way.

Acts of Love

When you discipline with the child's present and future welfare in mind, discipline is definitely an act of love. To that end, if you are so inclined, you can explain this part of your parental responsibility to your child by saying something like this: "Please know that I care enough to instruct and correct you for your own good, even when it causes you to feel I am a mean parent, to feel angry at me, and it causes friction between us. It's hard to face your disapproval when I raise issues you don't want to discuss. It's hard to make demands and set limits you resent when I take a stand for your best interests against what you want or like. But I love you enough to do so when I believe it is required. I know it's hard for you to believe, but I am on your side. I am not against you. Discipline is not something I do *to* you; it is something I do *for* you. It is not something I do to hurt you; it is something I do to help you. I do it for you now, and for your future."

At least in the moment, discipline can feel like thankless work. That's why taking a long view is important. In your child's adulthood, you will see some fruits of your steadfast labors to teach healthy habits. The child with whom you battled endless years to pick up a messy room emerges as a young person who likes to live in a clean and orderly space. The child who selfishly resented your demands to give help emerges as a young person who is extremely considerate of others. The child who required your continued insistence to accomplish homework becomes a young person with a strong and reliable work ethic. And you will think to yourself, "Maybe my efforts were worthwhile after all!"

Pressure to Be Perfect

Many parents (particularly those with only one child), wanting to be the best parents they can be, think the best is being "perfect." This belief is mistaken. Think about it.

Progress is a much more humane goal than perfection. Human is real. Perfection is ideal. In addition, if a child really had perfect parents, how would that child tolerate his or her own imperfections? The answer is, not very well. "I'm the only one in this family who ever makes mistakes! I'm the only one who does things wrong! I can never do things well enough!" Self-criticism of this kind can be abusive, the child ending up racked with guilt, or even filled with shame, for not measuring up to the family model. Better to have human parents who, even at their best, perform unevenly, acknowledging their shortcomings and admitting their frailties as they keep trying to do the best they can.

 **ESSENTIAL**

The only way to be a perfect parent is to have perfect children. And what loving parent would want to subject children to that kind of pressure—having to strive to reach unreachable standards, feeling obliged to live error-free, just to be okay?

So much of discipline, both instruction and correction, is directed at nurturing performance of one kind or another, it really helps if you can let the child know no one is perfect, including yourselves. You can use as a model the Great School of Life. "You know," you can say, "in the Great School of Life, we are all students. We never get to experience it all. We never get to learn it all. We never get to graduate. We never get it all right. We never learn it all on our first try. And a lot that we learn is from failure and mistakes. No student, ourselves included, gets all A's in the Great School of Life. The main thing is to show up to class every day and try to learn what you can. We never could do more than that ourselves, and we don't expect any more of you."

Keeping Priorities in Order

There are plenty of times when you set aside your individual needs for the moment to tend to the more pressing needs of your children. But over the long haul, your children should remain a third-order family priority.

Your first priority should be taking sufficient care of your individual needs so you can fully and freely respond to those of your spouse and children. For single parents, remembering this priority is particularly important since the welfare of your child depends on having a healthy and stable parent. Self-sacrificing for your children can, at some point, prove to be at the children's expense when the parent ceases to function well and begins to make bad choices. Hence the guideline: To take good care of your children, take care of yourself.

Your second priority should be giving sufficient attention to your marriage so that it remains strong. A strong marriage is important to the whole family. Parents who stop nourishing their relationship can become estranged and fractious with each other, and this conflict creates instability in the home. Tension between parents creates insecurity in children. Out of respect for the children, do not neglect the well-being of the marriage on which your children depend. Hence the guideline: To take good care of your children, take good care of your marriage.

Children are your third priority—not out of neglect, but out of respect for what it takes to create a healthy family structure around them. If you place the children as a continuing first priority, they will develop an unhealthy amount of influence, coming to dominate attention at the expense of others in the family. "Our children always come first" is sometimes claimed as a statement of positive parenting, when it is often not. With the individual well-being of each partner secured, and with the well-being of the marriage secured, the well-being of your children will be secured.

ALERT!

Partners can become so preoccupied with parenthood that they neglect to pay adequate attention to themselves and their relationship. Their undue absorption with the child can undermine their marriage.

CHAPTER 3

The Limits of Parental Control

S OME PARENTS SUBSCRIBE to the input/output theory of parental influence: Put in "good" parenting and a "good" (happy, healthy, and successful) child will result. Effort equals outcome, they believe, because quality of parenting makes most or all of the difference in how a child "turns out." This theory is partly true and partly false.

Parental Influence in Perspective

Certainly, parenting—the time and energy and loving dedication invested in one's mothering or fathering task—matters. However, many other factors also shape the course of a child's growth. Consider just a few sources of influence over which parents have no control. Parents don't control:

- *The culture into which the child is born or the onslaught of media messages that it sends*—the experiences it glamorizes, the ideals it presents, and the motivations it encourages.
- *The child's inborn characteristics*—the temperament, personality, aptitudes, and physical traits that genetic inheritance endows.
- *The choices the child makes*—the personal decisions that ultimately determine what he or she will or will not do.

- *The circumstances to which a child is exposed away from home*—the unfamiliar and challenging situations he or she gets into out in the world.
- *The child's companions and the pressures they can bring to bear*—the opportunities for risk-taking, for experimenting with adventure and the forbidden, that peers provide.
- *Chance events*—the play of luck that can favor, spare, or victimize a young person's life.

Since parenting is only one of many influences on a child's development, how your child "turns out" is not all to your credit or to your blame.

The Extent of Parental Responsibility

For you to take total blame for what happens (your child's substance abuse, for example) or for what is not happening (your child not studying hard enough to make the honor roll, for example) is giving too much credit to the power of parental influence. Expecting to have this much control over your children can lead to feelings of inappropriate guilt—parents punishing themselves for what they are powerless to control. Then the child, who cannot resist manipulating a guilty parent to escape personal responsibility, may declare, "It's not my fault for failing; it's yours for moving and making me change schools!" And the parent may believe it.

 **QUESTION?**

What is the extent of parental influence?
As a parent, you influence your child by the example you model (who and how you are), the treatment you give (how you choose to act and react with your child), the structure you impose (what you value and allow), and the education you impart (what information and instruction you provide).

As a parent, you need realistic humility. You need to say the following to yourself: "I am not all-powerful. I am not all-knowing. I am not perfect. I cannot fully protect my child any more than I can fully prepare my child. I can be right some of the time, but not all of the time. I can be sensitive to some of my child's needs, but not to all of my child's needs. I cannot always be at my child's side. I can inform my child's choice, but I cannot control that choice. I can be totally committed to my child's welfare, but I cannot totally ensure that welfare even though I wish I could."

The Dangerous Equation

Parents who assume responsibility for everything that happens to their child tend to believe in a false equation: parents = child. This equation ties the adequacy of parenting to performance of the child, essentially making the child's behavior—good or bad—a measure of how good your parenting has been.

ESSENTIAL

> To break the "parent = child" equation, repeat to yourself: "Good parents have good children who will sometimes make bad choices in the normal trial-and-error process of growing up."

Bound by this belief, when your child makes a bad choice, you must fault yourself: "What have I done wrong?" By asking this question, you immediately misappropriate some responsibility for the child's decision. It is better to hold the child fully accountable for choices made by making a clear separation of decision-making power. "My parenting is my responsibility, but your conduct is yours. A bad choice does not make a bad child any more than a badly acting child makes a bad parent." A full-faith, honest effort is the most you can make; that effort (not the outcome) is really all you can control. The child's behavior is no more the final measure of the parent than parenting is the sole determinant of the child's actions.

Cooperation Required

Sometimes, in frustration over their son's or daughter's opposition or misbehavior, parents will lament, "We can't control our child!" They will treat this lack of power as a problem, when it is not. It's a reality. They never did and they never will control their child. But they want to believe in the illusion of control because without it parental responsibility can feel overwhelming.

Parents want to believe they are in charge. When your infant fusses and cries, you pick up the child, rock her gently, and the sobs subside. Now your tendency is to think, "I was able to stop the child's crying." But that is wrong. For whatever reason, the child decided to stop crying. You were simply taking credit for the child's decision.

What you do control is your own conduct. Often, in response to your changed behavior, however, your child can decide to behave differently in ways you like or want. You have influence on the child's decisions, but not control over making them. Therefore, to influence your child, control yourself. To get your child to change what she is doing, ask yourself what *you* are doing or not doing that might be supporting the continuation of the problem. Then consider acting differently in order to encourage a different behavior.

 **FACT**

> Your behavior is not only the example that you model for your child to follow in the future, but it is also the behavior that influences how your child responds to you in the present. Each of your actions as a parent affects your child both now and later.

To Change Your Child, Change Yourself

Maybe if you lower your voice, de-escalate your anger, and start talking reasonably, your child will stop yelling, too. To influence your child to make a different choice instead of repeating the misbehavior, ask yourself: "What was I doing before, during, or after the problem occurred that I might change to positive effect?"

Sometimes, *asking* an independent child to do something works better than *telling* him to do it, because the request communicates respect. "When my parents ask me instead of tell me, I feel they are treating me as an equal. Orders feel insulting." Asking is a courtesy that acknowledges the child's choice and solicits cooperation.

However, sometimes you may get better results by *telling* an oppositional child to do something, rather than asking, because if she believes she has no choice, then there is no point arguing. Telling assumes your child's compliance. "If it's an order, then I know there's no room for discussion."

Getting out of Negative Cycles

If you find yourself repeatedly in a spot where you and your child both end up getting angry at each other, that is a sign that you and your son or daughter are stuck in an automatic, self-defeating pattern. You need to interrupt your pattern of reacting and create time to think.

Suppose, for example, for the past few weeks, you've been trying to get your daughter to go to bed at 8:00 P.M. She's not ready to go to bed, however, and she fights your efforts to enforce this bedtime. Because it is the end of the day and you are both tired, you both become emotional during your conflict and are unable to resolve it peacefully. Every night you're having the same, predictable argument. At about 7:30 P.M., you (and your daughter) can feel tension start as you anticipate the encounter you know is going to come at bedtime.

What can you do to try and get your child's cooperation? First, understand that when your child gets upset, her emotions take over her thinking. The same is true for you. When someone gets emotionally upset, for the moment there is no thinking person home. So, rather than allow feelings to continue to do your "thinking" for you, declare a timeout so both of you can cool down and allow the power of reason to solve the problem. Then say something like this to your daughter: "The way we are doing bedtime isn't working for either of us. We need to start over. We need to find a different way. Let's each think about what that might be."

For you, the first part of the answer is to not do whatever you have been trying, since that seems to be supporting the continuation of the problem. So, you must take a clear and honest look at your own "bedtime" behavior. You may find that your method is a combination of telling ("You will") and yelling when you don't get your way, the child telling ("I won't") and yelling back.

Ask your daughter why going to bed on time is so hard to do. She may reply, "I don't want to go to bed when you're angry at me. I feel scared. Maybe when I wake up you will still be angry with me!" To this you answer, "Well, I wouldn't get angry if you'd just go to bed when you are told!" But then you think about your own behavior and offer to work out a different bedtime scenario with her. "What could I do with you before bedtime that would cause you to feel warm and close to me?" Then your daughter does some thinking. "You could lie down with me and we could snuggle, and you could read me a story." And you agree to give this a try.

 **QUESTION?**

What if you can't figure out a way to stop a recurrent problem with your child?
Instead of treating the situation as your responsibility alone to solve, treat it as a mutual concern. Enlist the child's ideas to help solve the problem. Two heads are often better than one.

Building Blocks of Cooperation

Around ages three to four, your child should be trained in the basics of cooperation, learning skills that can be taught only through lots of repetition. Remember that repetition builds habits, and you want to build a habit of cooperation in your child so he or she will work with—and not against—you, now and in the years ahead. There are four building blocks of cooperation to teach your son or daughter.

- **Listening and attending:** "What did you hear me ask? Tell me what I just said." You want your child to be in the habit of tuning you in, not tuning you out. Your child thinks, "I know what you want when I pay attention to what you say."
- **Giving to get:** "What do I need you to do for me? Tell me what you do for me that gets me to do for you." You want your child to be in the habit of thinking about how her meeting your needs is connected with your meeting her needs. She thinks, "I do for you and you do for me."
- **Keeping agreements:** "What did you promise me? Tell me what you agreed that you would do." You want your child to be in the habit of keeping his word, not forgetting or breaking it. He thinks, "When I tell you I'm going to do something, I mean what I say."
- **Being of service:** "What special help can you provide? Tell me how I can call on you when I have need?" You want your child to be in the habit of valuing what he has to contribute to the family. He thinks, "I have skills worth offering."

Children who are taught early to listen, to give to get, to keep agreements, and to be of service to their parents—and who are rewarded with praise every time they do these things—tend to be more cooperative with their parents than children who lack these basic interpersonal skills.

Attention Disorders

Attention deficit disorder (ADD) describes a condition in which a child shows an inability to pay prolonged attention to a single task and is easily distracted. Attention deficit hyperactivity disorder

(ADHD) describes a condition in which a child shows an inability to stay still and needs to be in constant motion. Both terms are becoming increasingly common as diagnostic labels given to restless children with wandering minds when they misbehave or are particularly disruptive at home or, especially, at school.

In addition, there are often two "deficits" at work, not one. There is the inability to pay enough attention, and there is also the inability to *get* enough attention. Perhaps because these children receive so much negative adult attention, they hunger for positive attention even more. They are often "attention getters."

Parents and teachers often find ADD/ADHD children difficult to manage. Children who suffer from ADD/ADHD are constantly corrected and frequently punished by frustrated and angry adults, and they often internalize the negative treatment they are given by thinking of themselves in negative terms. "I'm bad." "I'm stupid." "I'm a troublemaker." "I'm a misfit." "I'm a loser." They see that adults view them like this, and they come to view themselves the same way. Such name-calling is used to justify treating themselves badly and only lowers their self-esteem.

Growing Up in an Overstimulating World

Consider the world of experience and play in which today's children grow up. For many parents it seems different from the one in which they grew up.

- Children are given more information about life and the larger world at a younger age than ever before.
- Children are growing up in a world with an ever-increasing rate of social, cultural, and technological change.
- Children's entertainment is increasingly sensational, violent, and quickly moving to excite interest and appeal to a short attention span.
- Children are given more consumer choices than they know how to make.
- Children are enrolled in more after-school activities than most of their parents ever were.

- Children are given more aggressive media advertising—promoting all that is new and different—than they can resist easily.
- Children are given more electronic forms of entertainment that require changing attention quickly and doing multiple tasks at the same time.
- Children are given more new toys and possessions than they can use.
- Children are exposed to more fad and fashion than they can keep up with.
- Children are becoming increasingly dependent on external sources of entertainment to escape boredom, becoming less able to entertain themselves.

Stimulation Overload

Given all the stimulation from information, entertainment, and sheer number of choices that children are given today, is it any wonder that they grow up in a state of stimulation overload? Is it any wonder that they become culturally conditioned to let their attention wander, to be restless, or to become easily dissatisfied? Is it any wonder that they have a fascination with novelty, a hunger for the new and different, a need to be occupied by multiple tasks, an intolerance for boredom, an aversion to routine, a disinterest in the old and the same, and a horror of inactivity?

Our society has created a disconnect between how children are conditioned by culture and how they are expected to behave at school—to sit still, to be quiet, to follow directions, to focus on one thing at a time, and to spend sustained time working on unexciting instructional tasks.

Discipline Through Medication

To what degree should your child's restless behavior and wandering attention be "controlled" through the use of medication? That is the question increasingly raised by parents and teachers in response to a growing population of children who are often inattentive, easily distracted, extremely impulsive, or constantly on the move. In any of these cases, such children prove difficult to "control" for the adult powers that be.

Why Medicate?

Unhappily, medication seems to be becoming the first resort, not the last, in many of these cases. Ideally medication would be given only after a host of other helping and self-management strategies have been given a fair try. The medication—usually psychostimulants—can in some cases slow impulsiveness and the tendency to be distracted and increase the child's ability to follow directions and remain focused on a single task.

 **ALERT!**

As with any medication, there are known risks of some side effects. But with medicines used to treat ADD/ADHD, there are also unknown risks associated with the effects of early psychoactive medication on the brain, later learning, and developmental growth.

On the positive side, many medicated children (as well as concerned adults) will report an improved ability to control impulse, to comply with directions, and to concentrate on tasks, which results in fewer cases of getting in trouble (with teachers, parents, or whoever may be in authority). In this sense, life with the ADD/ADHD child becomes easier and less troublesome for adults. For the child, as his disruptive behavior subsides (and more boys than girls are "diagnosed" with these disorders), his treatment by the adults around him improves.

But what you must consider as a parent is whether this increased compliance at home and at school is really what your goal should be with these children. Do you want to just adjust children's behavior with medicine to fit adult needs for conformity and control? There are other options.

To medicate or not to medicate your overactive or inattentive child may be the question you face as a parent. Although the research jury is still out on this, your answer needs to consider the possibility that by establishing some degree of dependency on a stimulant drug to manage her behavior now, you may affect her susceptibility to self-medicating with recreational drugs in the future. In addition, there is the risk of known and unknown side effects on your child's physical and psychological development. Therefore, it is wise to exhaust all other, nonpharmaceutical interventions before putting your child at risk in this way.

 **FACT**

> Just because psychoactive medication has reduced ADD/ADHD behaviors doesn't mean you should stop teaching your child how to control his impulses and pay attention. Use the break from problem symptoms to continue to teach your child how to develop more physical and social self-discipline.

Try Training Before Medication

A good starting point for dealing with ADD/ADHD without medication is occupational therapy. Children are taught, through hours of practice, individual self-management skills, and parents are taught effective ways to work with their child. With this help, your child can learn ways to focus on a task and follow directions and to manage fidgety energy and wandering attention. As parents, you can learn strategies to use at home for reducing distractions; channeling restless energy; and using structure, routine, proximity, and touch to help your child focus better and settle down.

Finally, ask yourself the question, "Are we giving this medication for our child's sake or for our own in order to temporarily make our parenting job, or the job of the school, easier?" Be honest with your answer. If the child's medication is as much for your sake, or for the teacher's sake, as it is to help the child, then medicating your child may not be the best choice. Reducing discipline problems associated with impulsiveness and inattention at home and at school is not a good reason to medicate your child without trying behavioral training (for both child and parents) first. Using prescription medication as a disciplinary intervention with a child sometimes creates dependent parents who believe they can't effectively manage their child without keeping him or her on psychoactive drugs.

Parents have a substantial amount of influence over their children, but they do not have control over them. Teaching your children to cooperate with you, instead of struggling against you, will help you raise children who abide by your values and follow your rules.

CHAPTER 4

The Principle of Consent

Y OU KNOW NOW THAT PARENTS can't control a child's decisions, so how can they guide their children's behavior? The answer is a kind of cooperation, and its name is consent. Consent is your child's willingness to go along with what you want and don't want to have happen, to heed your instruction, and to accept your correction. Recognizing consent and respecting the value of consent in your relationship with your children will help you see positive ways to discipline effectively.

Working for Consent

As parents, you are always working for consent, rewarding the child with appreciation and praise when you get it. Even when you have to remind your child ten times before he empties and refills the litterbox for the cat he begged you to get and promised to take care of, you sincerely (and without complaining about how many times you had to ask) thank him for getting the job done. Otherwise, he will likely complain in return, "You never appreciate what I do!" Children are more often correct about this than not. Most parents do not appreciate all the consent they are given.

The only time many parents seem to be aware of consent is when they don't get it. What a costly oversight! Since positive parental responses have so much more shaping power than negative responses, you should be rewarding consent with an expression of appreciation and praise every time you get it.

ESSENTIAL

To encourage cooperation, always reward your child's consent with expressions of appreciation.

Acknowledging Consent

For their child's sake and for their own sake, parents need to keep the larger picture of consent in view. Even the most willful, obstinate, and rebellious child gives some consent. He does some things that his parents want, and he avoids some things that he knows his parents don't want him to do. When a child feels her parents don't see all the consent that she does give, she feels unappreciated and unfairly evaluated. When parents believe they aren't getting any consent from their child, they feel frustrated and frightened.

The lesson is: Always recognize and credit the consent that your child gives you. This recognition will help you maintain a healthy perspective on the times when he refuses to give consent. It also encourages your son or daughter to continue giving his or her consent. Acknowledging to your child that you appreciate that he has done what you want him to do makes him feel that it is worth his effort to do so again. If you do not acknowledge these times, you may be in for a lot of encounters with an angry child who feels unappreciated, and you may begin to feel fearful that you've lost all influence.

Seeing the Big Picture

As a parent, you don't want to become overly preoccupied with the problems that you experience with your child's behavior. Problems are by definition negative—something the child is doing or not doing that is wrong in the eyes of the parent and needs to be corrected. Unfortunately, by focusing on what is going wrong, parents often lose sight of all that is going right.

Consider a parent who complains to a counselor that her child is completely out of control. "She refuses to get off the phone when I ask no matter how angry I get. I battle with her about this every night. She won't do anything I say! She's totally defiant!"

If the parent is correct, and the child is nothing but disobedient, the mother is indeed in a lot of trouble. But the parent is not right. She has just become fixated on an ongoing problem, allowing that fixation to take over her entire view of the child.

So in response to the parent's complaint, the counselor asks some clarifying questions. Does she get up all right in the morning for school? Does she come home at the hour you set? Does she do chores? Does she help out when you ask? Does she get her homework done without your supervision? Does she behave as you would like at school, at other people's homes, out in the world? By answering yes to each question, the parent begins to see that in the big picture, her daughter is by no means out of control, that she is, in fact, giving her parent an enormous amount of consent. Keeping sight of the big picture keeps passing problems in perspective.

ALERT!

> When parents believe their child is "nothing but a problem," that negative view can also discourage the child. "All I ever do is get in trouble." Parents should always look at a problem as a small part of a larger person who possesses lots of strengths to make things better.

Compromising to Get Consent

Consent is a compromise for parents. Mostly you get consent, but in some areas of the child's life, for some periods of time, you will not. Usually, if you will hang in there regarding the issue that's causing problems, being steadfast and not overreacting, your insistence will wear down the child's resistance over time. "There's no point in fighting my parents on something when I know they mean business, are not going to change their minds, and are not going to back off."

In times when your child doesn't give you consent right away, but rather delays doing what you asked him to do, you may, at first, feel frustrated. However, remember that resistance in families is often a double standard. You may believe it's okay for you but not for your child. Your child asks you for something right away and you say, "Not now, later," resisting because you've had a long day, are feeling tired, or are otherwise occupied. Your delay seems reasonable to you.

 **FACT**

How you treat your child is how you treat yourself. Yell at your child, and you have just treated yourself as a person who yells. Listen to your child's explanation, and you have just treated yourself as an attentive and patient person. The better you treat your child, the better you treat yourself.

But when you ask your child for something right away and in words or actions she communicates, "Not now, later," that resistance doesn't seem okay because it denies you, the parent, what you want when you want it. Your expectation is that your child will give you immediate attention out of respect for your parental authority. And by the same right of authority, when the tables are turned and you don't want to respond immediately to something your child wants, you believe your delay is justified because of your child's subordinate position in the family. To encourage your son or daughter to comply with your requests more quickly, however, sometimes you should practice more timely compliance with his or her requests, even when your first instinct is to delay.

Delay is always dismissive. When a person doesn't respond right away (whether it is the parent or child who is delaying), it says to the other person, "Your request matters more to you than responding to it means to me right now." Putting off someone's request can cause that person to feel unimportant, unless the delay is accompanied by a commitment. Thus, when you have to delay responding to a request by your child, it is often helpful to say, "Not now, but definitely later," and give a specific time when "later" will occur (for example, "after I finish my phone call"). You can use the same strategy when your child wants to delay responding to your requests. "If not right now, then you tell me exactly when." Then hold your child to the time agreed. Delaying a response and then never following up is really just a refusal in disguise.

Handling Frustration

Sometimes the reality of having to wait for or work for consent is more than parents can bear. They get frustrated at not getting their way right away, and they may explode at, threaten, or verbally attack their child. In the process, not only do parents often do or say things that they later regret, but also the child gets hurt and loses some trust in the safety of the relationship. In addition, he or she also gains a measure of unhealthy influence over the parent. The child ends up in control when he realizes he has the power to provoke his parents into emotional outbursts.

"But my child makes me so angry!" protests the frustrated parent. This is the wrong way to think about it. Your child cannot make you feel anything without your permission. If you believe your child can "make you" sad or angry, then you are giving up control of your emotions, blaming your child for your unhappy state. Never give this power away to anyone. Your child is responsible only for his actions. Only you are responsible for your emotional response.

It is normal for parents to feel frustrated knowing a child can choose to consent or not. Confronted with a difficult problem with their child, they may wish that they could control the child's decision-making, which is, they now know, impossible. But when they lose control trying to force control, the child usually ends up in control, and some injury is often done in the process.

 **ALERT!**

> Parents who lose their tempers when their children deliberately delay responding to a request are giving their children the power of provocation. The most effective parents are those who do not take resistance personally, who stick by their demands, and who refuse to get upset no matter how long it takes for their children to give consent.

Desperation Statements

To avoid unhappy emotional arguments, parents need to monitor their state of mind and what they are communicating. Parents often make statements out of desperation that show how frustrated they are feeling, which increases the likelihood of overreacting. A few of the more common desperation statements follow.

Statement parent makes in frustration: "I'm going to keep punishing you until your attitude improves!"
Why is it harmful?
If punishment is all you do, a more negative attitude is all you'll get.

Statement parent makes in frustration: "I'm going to keep taking things away until you do what I say!"
Why is it harmful?
Take away everything the child values, and he or she has nothing left to lose.

Statement parent makes in frustration: "You'll never learn!"
Why is it harmful?
The child just has not learned yet. Dooming the future provides little hope and poor incentive for improvement.

Statement parent makes in frustration: "You're nothing but a problem!"
Why is it harmful?
Any problem is only a small part of a large person, and parents should keep that larger perspective.

Statement parent makes in frustration: "You're just acting this way to make me look like a bad parent!"
Why is it harmful?
It's not personal—most children are too self-occupied to calculate how their behavior impacts their parents' reputation.

Statement parent makes in frustration: "You're ruining the family!"
Why is it harmful?
The child can't make the family unhappy without the cooperation of other family members. So responsibility for whatever unhappiness exists in the family needs to be shared.

Statement parent makes in frustration: "You're driving me crazy!"
Why is it harmful?
Take responsibility for your behavior. You are choosing to drive yourself crazy on behalf of your child's behavior and then blaming your choice on the child.

Isometric Encounters

Sometimes, when your child is giving you maximum resistance, refusing with all her might to do what you want, you may decide to show her who has the most power by pushing back with all your might. This creates an isometric encounter. What is isometrics? It is a strength-training procedure. The harder you push against something with strong resistance, the stronger you will become. Thus when you give your child maximum resistance to push against, you're giving him a chance to grow stronger.

"You will do what I want!"
"No, I won't!"
"Yes, you will!"
"You can't make me!"
"Yes, I can!"

"Try and you'll be sorry!"

And as you battle with each other, both resisting harder and harder, you may find a way to use greater emotional intensity or greater physical strength and win the encounter. But have you really won? Prevailing is not the same as winning. So you physically drag your daughter back to the dinner table and hold her in her chair, saying, "I told you that you are not allowed to leave the table without asking permission first, and I meant it!" Finally, she may stop struggling, but her clenched jaw and angry eyes give you another message. "Wait 'til the next time!" her defiant expression seems to say.

The lesson is: Never get into an isometric encounter with your child. Even if you prevail at the moment, you will lose over the long haul. Why? Consider three destructive results. She has isometrically strengthened her power of resistance by pushing as hard as she can against you, so she will be stronger in future encounters. She will be more stubbornly resolved than ever to challenge your authority again. And she will deeply resent you for the humiliation of her defeat.

 **QUESTION?**

What is the downside of using physical force to control your child?
Parents who rule by brute force and intimidation earn contempt for being adult bullies, not respect for being family leaders.

You should avoid isometric encounters. If your child is using everything he has to resist your demand at the moment, back off and wait until his intense emotions have subsided before you bring up the issue again. Let him know that the issue isn't going anywhere, and you are prepared to wait however long it takes to work through the disagreement between you without either of you resorting to emotional or physical force. The message to your child is, "You may delay giving consent with your resistance, but you will never make that issue go away because I will keep coming back to you with it until we reach a satisfactory resolution."

Some parents actually train opposition they don't want by fighting it every step of the way. "We've argued with him from day one about not arguing back when we tell him what to do, and now that he's a teenager he argues worse than ever. He won't give up, he won't back down, he won't change his mind, and he has to have the last word." Arguments create a situation in which the child learns to argue back with parents who argue to get their way. And repeated arguing teaches persistence—the child becomes more invested in arguing with every argument he makes. Be careful not to model the very behavior that frustrates you in your children by how you resist their resistance.

The Power of Choice

In a relationship, choice is power. The more choices you have, the more ways you have to influence the other person. If you have no choice, then you have no power.

Thus, in the beginning, your infant feels powerless. By comparison, you appear extremely powerful because you have so many choices as an adult to determine what the child can or cannot have and when he can have it, while the child has far fewer choices for ways to influence you. The discovery by the infant that two behaviors—crying and smiling—are connected with getting your attention begins to empower the boy or girl with a sense of influence in the relationship. From here forward, your child's growth is a process of gathering more power of choice as he or she journeys from dependence on you in infancy to independence of you as a young adult.

Your final goal as a parent is to work yourself out of a job, at last turning over decision-making responsibility for the conduct of his or her life to your grown child, who can live by independent choices (and not your own). Until then, you are using your power of discipline to help the child gather that responsibility in appropriate and constructive ways. To do this, you need to keep the upper hand by having more choices for influencing the child than he or she has for influencing you. You need to keep the power of most choices on your side. This proposal may sound easy to do because you are the adult and you control so much that the child wants, but it is not.

When Misbehavior Continues

Sometimes, in the normal course of your child's growing up, you will experience times when your child continuously misbehaves, defying all your disciplinary efforts. For example, you can't seem to get your daughter to stop throwing tantrums when she is denied something she wants. This is hard enough to deal with at home, but consider a tantrum she throws in the afternoon at the supermarket, with other shoppers staring. She screams, and none of your explaining, orders, or pleading gets you anywhere, and finally you let her have the candy you forbade her to have, and she quiets down immediately.

Your child got what she wanted—the candy. You got what you wanted—the end of the tantrum. But now your daughter knows that throwing a tantrum will get her what she wants—while you feel that by giving in, you are encouraging this misbehavior to happen again, which is true. "I tried everything!" you think. "I tried everything, but nothing works. I've just run out of choices. There's nothing I can do!" Who has the most influence now? A power reversal has taken place.

 **ESSENTIAL**

One way you can get your son or daughter to cooperate with you while still giving him or her a measure of control is to offer a choice within a choice. Say, "Here is what I want. Here are three ways you can make it happen. You can choose which way."

So what is the solution? First, you have to realize that you haven't tried *everything*. You have allowed frustration and discouragement over a hard problem to wear you down. What you have lost is the will to try. To get that back, reach out for social support from family or friends who can encourage you to keep on trying. Use that support to brainstorm and replenish your supply of possible disciplinary choices. No parent has ever "tried everything," because there are simply too many choices a parent can try. The most powerful disciplinary choice parents have is to keep trying different choices until they find a choice that seems to work, at least for a while.

A friend can offer some alternatives you didn't think to try. If your daughter throws a tantrum again in the grocery store when you tell her she can't have any candy, try singing a song to yourself. Try smiling and giving your child a hug. Try ignoring the noise and keep shopping. Try asking, "What fun thing shall we do when we get home?" Will any of these tactics work? Who knows? But at least you now have more options.

Children Need Choices, Too

The other side of the choice dilemma is the child's. Because parents control so many circumstantial choices in her life, a young child can sometimes feel as if she has no choice at all except to do what she is told. She can feel powerless and angry because of that, and may become resistant of her parents' requests in order to assert some measure of personal choice. This is what a lot of the child's resistance is about—gathering power of choice in a negative way.

Parents often become self-defeating at this point. They use punishment to take away further choice in the mistaken belief that this method will improve cooperation. But it won't. A resistant child needs *more* choices, not fewer.

Even though parents need to keep the most choices on their side, they need to be sure the child is given enough room for choice to be willing to cooperate with what parents want. Cooperation from the child requires allowing some self-determination for the child. For example, you tell the child what help you need, but within prescribed time limits, you let the child decide when to get the task done. "I would like you to mow the yard. Sometime this weekend before 3:00 P.M. on Sunday is fine with me. The exact time is up to you."

Giving your child a choice makes it easier for him to give you consent. You've showed that you respect him, and not only have you not lost any of your influence as a parent, you've actually increased it.

CHAPTER 5

Communicating with Courtesy

W HAT IS OFTEN TOO SMALL to appreciate when it is given, but usually too big to ignore when it is not? Courtesy—an old-fashioned notion that never goes out of style. Courtesy means using small acts of consideration to signify special caring for another person. It is crucial to effective discipline.

Why Courtesy Matters

"You never asked me!" complains the child. "What do you mean?" replies the parent. "I must have told you three times!" But the child is right. Being asked can feel much better than being told, because being asked is an act of courtesy. When you're requesting—rather than demanding—cooperation, you show that you aren't taking the child's cooperation for granted. To the child this courtesy conveys something big—respect. Being told is an act of command. It feels like being given an order with no choice but to obey.

To appreciate the power of courtesy, make a list of the qualities that you want to characterize your relationship with your child. For example, start at the beginning of the alphabet, with some *A* words. Suppose you would like "admiration," "approval," "appreciation," "affection," "attention," and "acceptance." Now ask yourself: How could these abstract qualities be conveyed? The answer is through small acts of courtesy that signify a lot.

- Praise signifies admiration.
- Compliments signify approval.
- Being thanked signifies appreciation.
- Being hugged signifies affection.
- Listening signifies attention.
- Being included signifies acceptance.

Small acts of courtesy represent larger values in relationships. In this way, little things can mean a lot. To be praised, complimented, thanked, hugged, listened to, and included cause both you and your child to feel good about your relationship. By the same token, because you are tired from work and your child is tired from school, you may each decide to let these small things go. So you are not thanked for remembering to pick up your child's school supplies, and your child is not listened to when she is describing a painful part of her day. If you omit courtesy, injury can occur because the neglected person feels wounded by the other person's insensitivity.

 **FACT**

When a significant courtesy has been omitted by your child, don't let it go. Brave appearing "oversensitive" or even feeling "foolish" and speak up about the slight you feel. Call attention to a lack of courtesy and you may get courtesy restored.

"Grace under pressure" is the ability to remember to treat other people with courtesy during times of duress. Courtesy is a very important discipline to learn because small acts of consideration have such a powerful impact on relationships, both when they are present and when they aren't.

The Power of Discourtesy

At worst, when you are under stress or preoccupied by problems with your child, you can commit acts of discourtesy that have enormously damaging effects because they communicate a significant lack of caring.

- Instead of praise, parents give the child contempt.
- Instead of compliments, parents give the child criticism.
- Instead of saying thanks, parents take the child's cooperation for granted.
- Instead of giving hugs, parents give the child no loving touch.
- Instead of being listened to, the child is ignored.
- Instead of being included, the child is excluded.

What's happened to the quality of the child's relationship with his parents now? While absence of courtesy can hurt, acts of discourtesy can do significant damage. It can actually injure your child's self-esteem. "You treat strangers who come to the door nicer than you treat me! And I'm your child. Aren't I worth treating nice, too?" And then parents wonder why their child has a negative attitude and is resistant to their requests.

Insisting on courtesy from your child counts for a lot because these small acts signify so much. If you and your children treat each other as guests in the relationship, the code of common courtesy is likely to be upheld. The quality of daily family life depends much more on each member's continuously observing minor courtesies than it does on how each person copes with the occasional major crisis.

 **ALERT!**

How you treat your child teaches that child how to treat you in return. If you want courtesy from your child, then practice courtesy yourself.

The Discipline of Apologizing

Hurt feelings happen. In the give-and-take between parents and child over the normal course of growing up, injury is sometimes given and received by both parties. Someone speaks an impulsive word, breaks an important agreement, tells a lie, forgets a significant commitment, or otherwise mistreats another family member. A sincere apology is important when either the parent or the child wrongs or hurts the other. Why? Because at issue is developing two important parts of discipline: conscience and self-correction. Apologizing serves several purposes after an incident of wronging or injuring each other has occurred. A sincere apology can encourage both you and your child to:

- Recognize the difference between doing right and doing wrong, and to subscribe to doing right. Sincere apologizing begins with the honest acknowledgment of how one has mistreated others.
- Own and admit culpability when giving injury or doing wrong. Sincere apologizing takes hard responsibility for one's actions.
- Feel genuine sorrow and appropriate guilt after hurting someone through ignorance, accident, or intent. Sincere apologizing is motivated by true remorse.
- Commit seriously to not repeating a wrong or injury that has just occurred. Sincere apologizing carries with it the firm intent to reform.
- Make amends by hearing out the wronged or injured party. Sincere apologizing means that there is no "statute of limitations" on feeling hurt from harm, and patiently commits to listening whenever and however long hurt from original harm continues to be truly felt by the other person.

You do not want to raise a child without a conscience, one for whom the distinction between right and wrong does not matter, or one who feels no remorse when wronging others. You do not want to raise a child who is determined to deny misdeeds or mistakes, or who stubbornly refuses to apologize for anything. You do not want to raise a child whose apologies are insincere, or who uses apologies as manipulation to escape consequences for wrongdoing.

And you do not want to raise a child who, after committing a wrong, stubbornly refuses to self-correct.

So how can you teach sincere apologizing? Apologizing must be modeled for it to be learned. Parents who refuse to admit wrongdoing encourage children to follow that example. It's worth remembering that parents can act badly just as children can. Parents can "shoot from the lip" when angry, for example, when caught off-guard by the unexpected, saying words they later wish they could retract. But done is done. "I'm sorry for what I said," the parent apologizes. "It was wrong to say what I did. My anger at what happened is no excuse. I won't ever say that again. And I am willing to hear about any hurt feelings my angry words have caused." Appreciating this honest expression of remorse and intent to reform, the child forgives the parent. "Thanks for saying you're sorry. I guess neither one of us does right all the time."

 **ESSENTIAL**

It's important for parents to keep a sense of humor. Laughter helps you appreciate perplexities you encounter, accept events you cannot change, and keep problems in perspective. Laughter helps you take lightly what matters seriously.

The Discipline of Forgiveness

Why forgive? The first reason the injured party needs to forgive, after receiving a full apology, is in order to let go of hurt that has been received. Holding on to hurt only nurtures grievance and encourages resentment. Additionally, forgiving allows the injuring party to let go of guilt. Holding on to guilt only continues self-punishment.

The Problem of No Remorse

Should you forgive a child whose actions have been hurtful to you but who expresses no remorse? "Since I didn't mean to hurt you, I have nothing to apologize for. How was I to know my getting into trouble at school would mean you had to leave work to come and get me out?" Or consider a different situation. "I don't agree with you that what I did was wrong. It wasn't like I was taking the car to do something social and didn't ask permission. You had no reason to worry. I was just taking it to the car wash and back."

Creating an Empathetic Connection

Should you forgive the unrepentant offender? Yes. But not before trying to help your erring child make some empathetic connection to how you were affected emotionally. Ask the child to reverse roles with you and see what that feels like. "So there you are, in the middle of an important meeting with your boss, and suddenly you have to leave work in order to help out your misbehaving child who is waiting in the principal's office to be picked up. What is your boss going to think of you for leaving like that? How are you going to feel about yourself for leaving?" Or in the other situation, reverse roles. "Suppose you came home, wanting to get on your computer to instant message your friends, only to find it wasn't there. How might you feel about it being inexplicably gone, and how might you feel when I returned it an hour later, explaining I had only borrowed it to show it to a friend? Would you feel all right if I had never asked you for permission?"

 **ALERT!**

How you treat your child teaches that child how to treat you in return. If you want courtesy from your child, then practice courtesy yourself. When you as a parent commit a wrong, own up to what you did or said, apologize and make amends, resolve not to repeat, and then forgive yourself. Ongoing guilt only erodes effective parenting. You will sometimes make damaging choices—that's how parenting is.

Particularly in adolescence, children can be so preoccupied with satisfying their own needs that they don't consider the effects of their actions on others. Many times, they don't intend to offend or injure, but they do. Apologizing in these two situations empathetically acknowledges that even thoughtless actions can have hurtful effects. Sincere apologizing helps the teenager become more emotionally sensitive to others.

Even after trying to get an empathetic connection, there will be times when you still feel hurt by a child who, after listening to your explanation, continues to truly believe he or she did nothing wrong. Should you still forgive if there is no remorse? Yes. For your own sake, you should still forgive the child. No good purpose is served by carrying an emotional burden while the young offender lives free of the hurt and anger. Do yourself a favor and let the grievance go.

When Not to Forgive

Are there times *not* to forgive? Yes. If after committing a wrong and apologizing for injury that was done, the child then goes out and repeats the same offense, further forgiveness would only make it easier for the child to continue or repeat the wrong behavior. Thus, in this situation, you declare, "The only sincere apology I will accept is not in your words but in your actions—never ever use that kind of language with me again!"

Finally, there is one category of wrongdoing you should never forgive—deliberate acts of wrongdoing committed with malicious intent. Malicious acts of harm are unforgivable and should not be forgotten so they will not be repeated. Just file them away and keep them filed away, as long as they do not occur again. "Threatening violence to your sister to take pleasure from her fear is absolutely wrong! We will not have any member of this family doing, or threatening to do, another family member deliberate harm. We will get help to stop the threat of violence and to heal the hurt. We will have a safe and fear-free home for every family member."

Malicious acts of wrongdoing must remain unforgiven to serve as painful reminders that what occurred must never happen again.

Communicating the Wrong Message

Parents have to beware of confusing their own self-interest with the interests of their child. They must be able to distinguish between wanting what is best for the child for the child's sake and wanting what is best from the child for the parents' sake. We live in a competitive society, and that competition can sneak into parenting and create problems. "How good I am as a parent is measured by how well my child performs and achieves." "The parent whose child does best, wins." Wins what? Social standing among parental friends? Bragging rights? "If my child does better than yours does, then I'm a better parent."

Competitive parenting exploits the efforts of children to enhance the standing of their parents. Parents, in an effort to satisfy their own ambitions, may subject their children to excessive pressure. "We just want the best for you" can communicate a different message to the child who knows that what it really means is, "We want the best *from* you."

 **FACT**

> To be a good parent, you don't have to do everything right. Like your children, you will make mistakes. A mixed performance is the best parents can give.

Parents invest a lot in their children, and they may feel that because of their sacrifices and contributions, they deserve high performance from their child in return. "If we give up for you, then you give back to us." At-home parents who invest all their time and effort in childrearing often get trapped into judging the adequacy of their own performance as a parent by the performance of their children. What other worldly measure of their own performance can they use? The answer is: enjoyment of and respect for the effort they make, and not the outcome they get.

Parents who feel insecure may also base their self-esteem on the performance of their child. Burdened by this dependency (which feels like a responsibility) the child may be taught his or her performance has direct bearing on the parent's sense of well-being and even social reputation. "We're proud of you" communicates not parental satisfaction with the child so much as how their personal pride depends on how the child performs. "The better you do, the better we feel about ourselves." (A better way to congratulate a child is: "Good for you!")

To make matters worse, parents who depend too heavily on their children for their self-esteem are often personally threatened when the child's performance fails, because this failure feels like a direct reflection of their own failures. Taking the unhappy outcome personally, they may respond in anger: "You've let us down!" And now the child has two problems, not one. First, the child must recover from his failure, and second, he must help restore the injured well-being of his parents.

At the very worst, parents may attack the problem by attacking the child: "You have really disappointed us." This can make a child feel guilty for hurting her parents and worry that good standing with her parents has been damaged, threatening the child's security and driving down self-esteem. All children need to be assured: "How you perform will not affect our love for you."

Adjusting for Growth Cycles

How you communicate best with your child depends partly on how receptive he or she is to you, which means understanding that there are growth cycles that every child goes through. Understanding these can help make your communication more effective.

It's a phrase you've probably heard to describe a young child at a particularly hard-to-manage age: "He's in his terrible twos." What's so terrible? For parents, the child seems more contrary, more curious, and more committed to following his inclinations. This is a change from the more docile and tractable person he so recently used to be. Now he's insisting on doing what he wants and getting what he wants, and when you get in his way, he lets you know he doesn't like the opposition you provide. He wants to go where you don't want him to go. He wants to climb where you don't want him to climb. He wants to play with what you want left alone. He is frustrated and angry with you a lot of the time, and it is easy for you to feel frustrated with him. You've just got him disciplined the way you like and now the training structure you've established is being contested. What's going on?

About every couple of years (from age two through adolescence), a new growth cycle seems to occur. Your child becomes discontented with the limits of freedom you've established for her. Growth cycles begin by the child's breaking the traditional boundaries that circumscribed allowable behavior, to create more room to grow. This is the child's job—to push for further growth when he or she feels ready. Your job is to restrain this push within the limits of safety and responsibility. It is this conflict of interests that is activated at the beginning of every major growth cycle—your child pressing for new terms on which to live, you insisting that many of the old terms still apply.

For example, your two-year-old (as thrilled by the mobility of walking as your sixteen-year-old is with being able to drive a car) believes he should be able to go wherever he wants, whenever he wants. As parents, you insist on teaching the child to manage this new freedom responsibly. You do not allow him to run anywhere he wants outside, any more than you let the sixteen-year-old drive wherever and whenever she wants.

How Growth Cycles Work

Growth cycles unfold in three phases. The first is disintegration. Disintegration begins when the child becomes sufficiently dissatisfied with her current place in life to begin breaking old boundaries of prescribed conduct. It's like the child is saying to herself, "I am no longer content with the restrictive terms on which I have been living." At this beginning stage of the cycle, the child may become more oppositional for parents to live with, and they are at risk of becoming angry in response. "You're not observing the rules you have been taught!"

The next stage—exploration—begins when the child, now eager to discover new ways of acting, uses the new freedom he has gained to experiment with different behaviors. At this middle stage of the cycle, the child can become more unpredictable for parents to live with, and they are at risk of becoming anxious in response. "We can't tell what you are going to try next!"

 **FACT**

Growth cycles are a healthy part of development and should be expected to create discipline problems as your child pushes for new terms on which to live, some of which will be acceptable to you and some of which will not.

The third stage is consolidation, and it begins when the child, now desiring to get new growth under control, incorporates the new behaviors into a new self-definition. It's like the child says to herself, "I like what I have gained and how I have become." At this final stage of the cycle, the child becomes more consistent for parents to live with, and parents are at risk of their relief's denying the inevitability of more growth cycles to come. "Thank goodness that's over; now we can relax."

Growth Cycles and Discipline

Each time a growth cycle occurs, your existing disciplinary structure will be tested at the beginning and somewhat modified by the end. As your child changes with healthy growth, you will change your disciplinary structure in response—less than the child wanted, but more than you had planned. That's the compromise of child raising.

Getting your needs met as parents often means modifying your communication somewhat, depending on where your child currently is in her growth cycle. Generally speaking, if your child is filled with stage one (disintegration) opposition, you should declare your needs: "This is what I need to have you do"; "Now is the time for doing what I said." There's little point in asking an oppositional child, "Would you like to?" Given a choice, the child's answer at this stage of the growth cycle will probably be "No." So don't give the oppositional child an obvious choice.

However, when your child is in stage three (consolidation) consistency, asking is often a better way to get cooperation than demanding is. Feeling more content, the child is usually more eager to work with you, glad to be back in your good graces for a while again.

Courteous communication between parent and child is essential to positive discipline. It is a major contributor to your quality of family life.

CHAPTER 6

Dealing with Differences

I F ALL CHILDREN WERE THE SAME, developing a discipline strategy for the whole family might be easier. And if both parents saw eye to eye on everything, they might find it easier to make discipline decisions together. And if your children were just like you, you'd know exactly how to handle them. But, of course, this is not the case.

Parents should expect diversity—between themselves, between them and their children, and between their children. A rule that makes sense to one parent may not feel right to the other. What works with one child may not work well with another. It is this natural human diversity that makes discipline more complex.

Multiple Children, Multiple Personalities

With some children it takes a lot of discussion and effort on your part before they will give their consent and accept discipline. Other children prefer being obedient to taking the time and effort to resist or fight your rules. Some children like to argue with correction, while others are reluctant to speak up. Some children demand to know your reasons, while others will accept rules without many questions. When it comes to discipline, "different strokes for different folks" is a fitting cliché. Every child is different from every other.

That's why one of your first jobs as a parent is getting to know this stranger who has been born into your care. What temperament, what sensitivities, what aptitudes, what personality does this little person possess? Just because your first child was docile and nondemanding doesn't mean that your second child will be the same way.

The parents of this child can still have the same family rules and values for both children, but the way they assert and enforce that discipline will have to be different with each child. Parenting is an art, and the art of early parenting comes down to this.

- You must learn the human nature of this stranger born into your care so he or she begins to feel understood by you.
- You must learn to accept this new child's human nature so he or she feels welcomed by you.
- You must learn to lovingly connect with the human nature of this child so he or she feels securely bonded with you.
- You must learn how to "dance" with the human nature of this child so you can lead the boy or girl in how to grow, and he or she can learn to follow your lead.

QUESTION?

Does positive discipline mean treating all your children the same way?
No. Although you may have the same disciplinary code—or values—with all your children, you will have to vary your disciplinary approach based on each child's temperament and personality traits.

Within the first three or four months of your child's life you should have some sense of his or her temperament (calm or excitable, for example), sensitivities (comfortable or uncomfortable with touch or noise, for example), aptitudes (quickly or gradually responds to visual or spoken cues, for example), and personality (seems quiet or sociable, for example). Your first job is understanding the individual makeup of the little person you are going to have to work with as a parent.

Not a Chip off the Old Block

In addition to having different personalities from one another, your children also have different personalities from *you*. It is easier for parents to understand and relate to a child who is, by nature, similar to them than to relate to a child who is different from them. For example, suppose your nature is to be calm, focused, quiet, introverted, thoughtful, and controlled, and you have a child whose nature is be excitable, distracted, loud, outgoing, emotional, and impulsive.

For the sake of your personal comfort, you might feel like trying to change the child's temperament to suit your own. "I've got to get him to slow up and quiet down." Unfortunately, inborn traits such as these are not easily changed, and your efforts to change them may feel like a form of rejection to your child. The risk is that the child may come to believe, "There must be something the matter with me because I am not exactly like my parent. I am not okay the way I am."

These feelings of rejection can become the basis for significant self-esteem and relationship problems later on. "I could never please my parent, no matter how I tried. I've always known something is wrong with me. I've always been a misfit—the family failure." It's important that you work *with* your child's personality style rather than struggling to change it.

Two Parents, Two Views

All families have systems of beliefs, with no two families sharing all the same rules and values. Each family also has its own disciplinary code. In two-parent families, that code is a combination of rules and beliefs that each parent deems important. And since each parent comes from a separate and distinct family background with different childhood experiences, all marriages are to some degree cross-cultural. This means that putting together a unified disciplinary approach will require understanding, accepting, and bridging the traditional differences that each brings to the marriage.

Joining Two Sets of Values

When you wed as partners, you had to determine on whose terms, according to whose rules and values, you were going to conduct your marriage. How was responsibility going to be shared? How were disagreements going to be worked out? Whose traditions would you celebrate or re-create on special occasions? A lot of work in early marriage is learning how to successfully bridge differences through listening and understanding, and how to resolve conflicts through concession and compromise.

When you have your first child, you have to remarry as parents. You begin to discover and determine how you want to function as a family. Now you find that you have different ideas about parenting that had never surfaced before.

 **FACT**

Having different values than your spouse regarding parenting is not a problem. It's a reality. Treat differences not as a source of divisiveness, but as a source of richness and strength. Two of you are wiser than one because your two points of view offer a broader vision than a single one.

Consider how easily parenting can complicate a marriage. Your infant is fussing in the other room. You want to pick him up immediately and hold him in order to make him feel secure. But your spouse thinks that he should be left alone to fuss, so that he doesn't become spoiled by indulgence. So, whose disciplinary values are right? You both are, because a value, by definition, is the belief that one is right about something.

If you choose to argue about whose value is correct, you will each only feel more "right" than before as you defend your respective beliefs. In fact, neither one of you has any business trying to change the other's values. To do so only damages the relationship. It sends a message of rejection: "Your belief is unacceptable to me!" And the argument becomes polarized: "I am as right as you are wrong!"

Resolving Value Conflicts

So what should you do when a conflict over disciplinary values arises? First, respect your partner's values. "We judge this situation differently, and that's okay." Second, specify each person's "wants." You want to pick up the infant right away. Your spouse wants to let the child learn to tolerate some mild discomfort. Third, without challenging or criticizing the value differences, negotiate a compromise of wants. So you agree on a time limit, after which if the fussing continues, you will go in and pick up the infant.

Value differences between parents over discipline, how to instruct and how to correct, will continue over the course of your parenting. Often, gender differences will be a factor—you may want to give different treatment to a child of the same gender as you. "You don't know what it's like to be a girl, but as a woman I do! Girls need more time talking on the telephone to friends than boys do," a mother may say. Likewise, a father may claim his own special understanding of his son because they are both male.

 **ESSENTIAL**

> Leave the value differences alone between parents. You don't have to convince your spouse that the reasons behind your values are valid. You just have to reach a compromise about what each of you wants the result to be.

Part of your commitment to each other as parents is to communicate for however long it takes to reach a disciplinary decision you can both live with and support. And part of your authority as parents is presenting a united front that cannot be divided and exploited by a manipulative child. Dealing with the child's misbehavior should always be secondary to reaching a joint decision that unifies and strengthens the marriage. The main rule to remember is never let parenting differences or decisions over discipline become divisive of the marriage.

Giving Acceptance versus Making Demands

Because love is based on giving acceptance, and training (where discipline occurs) is based on making demands, parents often vary in which of these two parenting components they are most comfortable providing. You may find it easier to give acceptance, which is appreciated by your child, than to make demands, which often are not. Or you may find it easier making demands than accepting changes that are part of your child's normal growing up.

If you are prone to be a high-accepting parent, you may have to work to develop your demanding side—setting limits, stating requirements, and confronting hard issues. If you are prone to be a high-demanding parent, you may have to work to develop your accepting side—listening, compromising, and tolerating differences.

If one parent, in an effort to avoid conflict, tends to give most of the acceptance, and the other parent, in an effort to control, tends to make most of the demands, this difference can create a divide in the marriage. "You never show love to the kids, all you do is order them around!" "Well, you never get after the kids to behave; you leave all the unpopular parenting to me!" Whether you're raising children alone or with a partner, you need to have both accepting and demanding sides of your parenting in working order.

Different Genders

Being the only woman in a household of men (when you have only sons), or the only man in a household of women (when you have only daughters), can also cause tension as you try to make equitable decisions about discipline. Sometimes, in this kind of family system, you may feel like a minority in the family because of a strong gender-based culture in the family. You may feel excluded or put down because of this difference.

You may hear things like, "How can a mother understand her son's needs as a man? As his father, I know best." It can feel like they are ganging up on you. Put down in this fashion, you can be denied full participation in parental decision-making. You can be treated as an outsider, excluded from the loop of information in which everyone else is often included. Or a daughter confides to her mother, "I'll tell you, if you promise not to tell Dad—he wouldn't understand." As you lose credibility with your children for being of a different gender, you are told less; as you are told less, you lose credibility for knowing less. In the end these behaviors can marginalize your importance in the family.

 **ALERT!**

Don't let your worth as a person and parent be diminished because you are a gender minority of one. You will lose self-esteem, your spouse will lose an equal partner, and your children will lose the benefit of your full influence and participation in their lives.

In such situations, the parent who shares the same gender identity with the children is often given more confidence, respect, empathy, authority, and support by them than the other parent. Sometimes it may feel like being loved *in spite of* your parental designation and not because of it. And when you protest, you can be accused of being oversensitive.

To have the children and the spouse you love treat you as a second-class parent because of your gender can hurt. You are being neither equally valued nor equally included. So what is to be done? Don't allow this kind of family discounting or exclusion to go unchallenged. Even in the most trivial of family affairs, assert your position as a parent of equal importance. Don't allow yourself to be put down. Don't allow yourself to be kept out.

The Danger of "Good" and "Bad"

Sometimes in families with two children, the first will seem naturally similar in nature to parents and be comfortably inclined to live up to their expectations, to agree with their values, and to comply with what they want. To this "easy" child, parents give a lot of approval and very little correction because very little is needed. The second child, however, is perhaps determined not to be a clone of child number one, and is perhaps vested with a more stubborn and independent nature. Because of this, he fails to meet certain parental expectations, rejects some of their values, and opposes a lot of their wants. To this "hard" child, parents give more disapproval and correction because more correction is needed.

Over time, parents find themselves modifying their labels for the children, the easy child now perceived as usually "good" and getting more positive attention for being a pleasure, and the hard child now often seen as "bad" and getting more negative attention for being a troublemaker.

Although the parents never say the terms "good" and "bad," the terms are sometimes used by the children themselves, who develop an envious relationship with each other. "You're so good, you get all their appreciation and I get none!" "Well, you're so bad, you get much more of their attention than I ever do!" So the good child becomes a magnet for compliments and rewards, and the bad child becomes a lightning rod for conflict and punishment. And the more fully each occupies his or her respective role, the more each feels prohibited from trying each other's role.

At the end of adolescence, which child is worse off, do you suppose? If you guessed the bad child, you are wrong. Now the bad child can admit being hard to manage, make amends, honestly declare, "You have known me at my worst," and with relief begin to let the good side out. The good child, however, often feels trapped by perfection, fearing that to let any bad side out would break that image on which parental love depends, and so with resentment carries on in an exemplary and unhappy fashion. "If I let myself act badly I would lose your love."

Every child needs permission to be both "good" child and "bad," to let both sides out. Thus, if you have children who are beginning to occupy these opposing roles, try to liberate them if you can. To the child in danger of going all "good," declare, "You know, if you do something we don't like or disagree with, that doesn't mean you're bad or that we'll love you any less. It just means you're human like everybody else, like us, sometimes acting to other people's liking and sometimes not."

 **FACT**

Some adolescents are too good for their own good. They are so concerned with maintaining a harmonious and pleasing relationship with their parents that the abrasive work of separation, experimentation, and independence is left undone. This can create a delayed crisis in early adulthood or even in midlife as they try to deal with independence and individuality for the first time.

And to the child in danger of going all "bad," declare, "You know, there is much more about you that we love and value than that we disapprove of. Just because we fight a lot over differences doesn't mean all you do is get into trouble. We believe the good in you far outweighs any trouble you might sometimes get into."

Differences between parents (who give discipline differently) and diversity between children (who receive discipline differently) can make it challenging to provide the necessary correction and instruction. The trick is to accept and work with the inevitable human differences that exist in every family.

CHAPTER 7

Parental Authority

AUTHORITY IS THE FOUNDATION on which your discipline depends. Without respect for your authority, your child is not likely to give consent to what you want—at least not without a lot of struggle. His respect for your authority can be based on love, so that your child goes along with what you want because he values you and your relationship. Or that respect can be based on fear, so that your child dreads knowing what will happen if he or she doesn't go along with what you want, because of the hurt you might inflict.

Fear-based authority can be costly to your relationship. Children learn to use distance, distrust, and deception as strategies to keep the scary authority at bay. If you want a close and trusting relationship with your children as they grow, do not resort to threat, force, or intimidation to get your disciplinary way. Instead, create a safe relationship of loving value that your child can truly respect.

Why It's Important

Your child must give you consent—that is, agree to do what you say—for your authority to take hold. However, parents should not ask their child for permission to be granted this authority in the family. Parents must assume authority if they expect it to be given. They must act like they are entitled to it. They must act in charge. They must expect to be respected, asserting authority in a manner that encourages the child's respect—not by abusing the power of their position.

The influence of your authority is less dependent on your power to dole out positive or negative consequences than you might think. It's more a matter of conveying a firm and confident attitude: "I mean what I say, and I will do what I can to help you behave responsibly." This attitude communicates the firm belief that, among other responsibilities, your job is to establish and enforce rules for the safety and well-being of the child, and that those rules shall be obeyed.

 **FACT**

> A family is not a democracy with elected leaders, where each family member has an equal vote. A family is a loving autocracy, where those with caretaking responsibility—the parents—are in charge of governing those who are dependent on their direction and support—the children.

A parent who just wants to be his or her children's friend, or who feels insecure or uncomfortable assuming authority, is soon going to be exploited by children who come to understand how much power they have in the family. Unable to set effective limits and to make effective demands, this parent increasingly lives by the children's terms. Children now set the behavioral agenda in the family by dictating wants or threatening upset if their wants are denied. The parent tries to please, tiptoeing around unpopular issues, not wanting to upset the children, indulging them to avoid conflict, placating them to keep the peace. This is the worst-case scenario—when a parent is unable or unwilling to assume authority.

The Dangers of Not Having Authority

Why would parents not assume authority? Some people grew up with such stern or harsh parental authority that they go to the other extreme to avoid inflicting similar suffering on their child. "I don't want to do to you what my parents did to me." Some people fear asserting adult authority because it creates inequality with their child. "I don't want to be your boss if it gets in the way of being your friend."

Some parents crave their child's approval. "I can't stand your being displeased with me." Others lack the confidence to assume adult authority. "I don't know how to take tough stands and make them stick." There are also parents who never had a model of effective parental authority to follow. "My parents were totally hands off—they never made me do what I didn't want and never stopped me from doing what I did."

QUESTION?

Do parents have to assume authority in the family?
Yes. Without parents assuming and exercising governing authority, there is no family structure of rules to limit freedom and to prescribe responsibility that children can depend on to grow safely.

By not assuming meaningful authority, parents risk encouraging their child to gather more power to control himself and the family than is healthy. Parents risk eroding their own effectiveness and self-respect as parents. They also risk shaping a self-centered child who may have problems accepting healthy limits in relationships and abiding by normal social rules.

Authority is part of the leadership that comes with the job of parenting—directing parts of the child's life, enforcing adherence to those directions, and gradually turning over more power of authority as he or she grows older and learns to direct himself or herself responsibly. This, of course, is the parents' ultimate objective: to put themselves out of the parenting business when the adult child is ready to assume responsibility for becoming the governing authority in his or her own life.

Establishing Parental Authority

If you feel uncomfortable asserting authority, can you learn to exercise this responsibility? Yes. You can practice a number of simple authority behaviors that all communicate that you are in a position of authority. Simple acts of authority include:

- Requesting information or asking questions about the child's life: "I want to know."
- Confronting issues in the child's life that you want to discuss: "We need to talk about this."
- Making demands for actions to be taken: "You need to do the following before you go."
- Setting limits on freedom: "You're not allowed."
- Expecting that agreements and promises be kept: "I will hold you to your word."
- Repeatedly insisting that an activity be accomplished: "I will keep after you until you get it done."
- Applying consequences (both positive and negative): "You have to work off the damage that you did."
- Advising the child on the best course of action: "In my opinion, this is what you need to do."
- Controlling what kinds of support you will give and what kinds you won't: "We won't buy you those kinds of clothes."
- Making judgments about what is going right and wrong in the child's life: "In our judgment, you handled that situation very well."
- Creating conditions on which freedom is based: "What we allow you to do partly depends on getting accurate and adequate information about what is going on in your life."

By practicing behaviors such as these, with sincerity and without backing off, parents will establish their authority.

Do not use threats to assert your authority. A true threat inspires fear, while an empty threat is like a broken promise. It causes the child to lose trust in your word. Commitments work better than threats: "If you choose not to do what I asked, then I will do what I said."

Authority That's Positive

Authority is not just about correction. Another side of authority is contributive. As a parent, you exercise contributive authority by providing positives in your child's life that you control—resources, permissions, encouragement, help, support, advocacy, protection, knowledge, instruction, coaching, and praise, for example. Generally speaking, the more you have to correct, the more you should also demonstrate the positive, contributive side of your authority. Otherwise, your child will begin to feel that your authority is all negative, when it is not.

Contributive authority is particularly important in second marriages where one partner is now stepparent to the other's child. Before the stepparent even thinks of exercising corrective authority, he or she should establish a base of contributive authority with the stepchild. In the beginning, the biological parent should be the one providing any correction. The stepfather or stepmother needs time to build up a solid base of positive authority before beginning to enforce corrective discipline. If the stepchild has been given no positive authority on the part of the stepparent to accept, then he or she is unlikely to accept the negative.

 **QUESTION?**

Can a parent regain authority once it has been lost?
Yes. Just put your child on the reactive by initiating more authority behaviors. The message these actions send is, "So long as you live with me, you have to live on my terms."

Authority Styles

How you position your authority—whether approachable or absolute—can make a big difference in your relationship with your child.

What's the Difference?

For the approachable authority, all rules are open for discussion, reasons or values behind them available for examination, arguments to the contrary listened to, and all questions answered, with the understanding that, like it or not, the parent still has the final say.

For the absolute authority, the child's speaking up may be considered "talking back," complaining considered "criticizing," questioning considered "disrespect," and arguing considered "defiance." Absolute authority believes the child should have no say.

Parents have to decide how approachable ("I'm willing to listen") or absolute ("My decision is not open for discussion") they want to be. By allowing the child to comment on and disagree with disciplinary decisions, approachable authority encourages active, independent thinking: "I speak up when I don't think my parents are being fair."

One risk for children socialized with approachable authority in the home is developing an attitude that they are entitled to argue with any outside authority with whom they disagree, and that may get them in difficulty out in the world. For example, an empowered only child (used to being treated like an equal by parents) may question a teacher's classroom rules and be sent to the office for insubordination. Approachable parent authorities can encourage children to speak up, discuss, question, disagree, argue, and not take an initial no as the final answer.

Problems with Absolute Authority

Absolute authority shuts down discussion and dissent, encouraging instead a passive and automatic obedience: "I do whatever my parents tell me, no questions asked." One risk of being socialized to absolute authority in the home is that children may learn that they should follow social directives from any outside authority without question. For example, they may do what a stranger tells them to do, even if it feels wrong, because that stranger is an adult. Absolute parent authorities can encourage children to shut up, give in, go along, and not think about the merits of what is being demanded of them.

A further problem with exercising absolute authority is that it can suppress normal adolescent desire to experiment with the forbidden, rebel against expectations, and risk independent action. Then the child's first experience of freedom from parental authority causes the child to try everything and anything, and he may make a host of bad choices. So the late adolescent, liberated from automatic obedience at home, decides college is the time to "act crazy" at last.

ESSENTIAL

Most parents alternate between absolute and approachable authority, depending on the situation. For example, stressed by demand, pressed by time, or faced with an emergency, they may decide that being absolute in their authority is more appropriate than being approachable.

In general, approachable authority has less of a downside than absolute authority, particularly once the child enters adolescence and has become more resistant to being managed by his parents. Then, approachable authority can offer a compromise that often works well: The child gets to have his say, but the parents get to have their way. Giving your child a chance to voice objections allows him to feel that he's standing up for himself, even though he ultimately consents to what you want him to do. "Okay, I'll help wash the car before going over to my friend's."

Ways You Communicate Authority

Whether you take an absolute or an approachable position, how you communicate the intent of your authority also makes a difference. You can use concern-based communication or control-based communication.

Concern- versus Control-Based Communication

Concern-based communication makes it clear that the parent is focused primarily on the child's welfare and well-being. You are saying, "Concern for you is my motivation. I don't want you to go to this event because of the risks involved. I'll tell you what they are as I see them. We can discuss them if you want. As your parent, I don't want to send you into a situation with a high likelihood of your getting hurt." You focus on expressing how much you care for the child's well-being.

Control-based communication suggests, however, that the parent is focused primarily on regulating the child's life. You are saying, "Control over you is my motivation. I'll tell you what you can or cannot do. I've decided you can't go to this event. There will be no discussion. You will do what I say. I will get my way."

Why Showing Concern Works

In general, children often respond better to authority that is communicated more out of concern for the child than control for the adult. Perhaps this is because the concern-based parent seems to be more on the children's side, compared to the control-based parent, who seems to be more against them. Concern-based communication also allows children to get into a dialogue with parents over the issue of disagreement or the problem to be solved, respecting their ideas, showing interest in what they have to say, even working out a solution or resolution that benefits from ideas the children have to offer. In concern-based communication, children are given some participation in the deliberation. In control-based communication, they are not.

Of course, there are times when control-based communication can be just what the child needs and even wants. For example, if your early adolescent is feeling unable to say no to a gang of friends who are egging each other on to commit some kind of mischief, you may intervene with instructions that seem more controlling to help extricate your child from the peer-pressured situation. "This is what you will do. You are to come directly home from school and not hang out. Any of these friends, one at a time, is welcome to come and play with you over here so long as I am present and our house rules are respected."

ALERT!

Even though *you* know that you are concerned for your child's well-being, using control-based communication doesn't always convey that message to the child. Often the child sees only your desire for control and resents or resists what seems just an assertion of parental power.

Explaining Your Reasons

Authority demonstrates the dominance of parents and the dependence of the child. This distinction becomes harder for your child to accept as she enters adolescence and begins her journey toward independence, toward finally living on her own terms.

"I should be free to live my own life, to do what I want, not what I'm told!" your twelve-year-old exclaims in frustration with your restraints. "You're not the boss of my world! Why do I have to do what you say? Just tell me why!" You may reply, "It's the parent principle. It's part of what mothers and fathers are supposed to do. I may not like it. You may not like it. But it's my job—making rules for you to follow and making them stick."

Should your child want more discussion, explain how no one, adults included, lives free of authority. Point out how outside of the family (at work and in society) there are more rules and people to enforce them. Your goal is to help your son or daughter learn enough about getting along with your authority at home to be able to work with all the authorities he or she will encounter in the larger world. In the family, exercising authority is part of your responsibility as a parent.

CHAPTER 8

Family Rules

HAVING ESTABLISHED FAMILY RULES to follow provides both essential training for your child at home and essential preparation for learning to follow social rules out in the bigger world. Rules provide structure for your children (and you) to use to make decisions about what should and should not be done. However, as with most things, the way rules are applied makes all the difference in their effectiveness.

Stemming from Worry

To some degree, your rules are sources of worry for you because many are put in place to keep your child safe from dangers that he or she may not foresee. The parents who are most ridden by worry tend to have the most rules.

"What if I make a wrong decision?" wonders the new parent. Parents make a lot of "wrong" decisions, but most children still come out all right. The challenge of parenting is making a full-faith effort, making mistakes in the process, self-correcting when you can, and learning as you go, developing your parenting one child at a time, because all children are different from each other.

What Is Worry?

What is worry, anyway? Worry is ignorance plus anxious questions plus fearful answers. Worry begins with ignorance: "I don't know why my child isn't home by the time we agreed on." Ignorance is made threatening by asking an anxious question: "What if my child has gotten into trouble?" Jumping to a fearful answer or conclusion completes the worry: "My child has probably been in a terrible accident!" One formula for worry is:

WORRY = "I DON'T KNOW" + "WHAT IF?" + "JUST SUPPOSE."

To keep worry down, it helps to accept ignorance or take action to reduce it. "As a parent, there will always be infinitely more I don't know (or control) about my child and my child's life than I can ever know, but when I have a need to know that can be satisfied, I will check it out."

It also helps to refrain from asking anxious questions. "As a parent, it is easy to wonder for the worst when I don't know; but I can refuse to scare myself on behalf of my child by refusing to create fearful possibilities to consider." And avoid giving fearful answers to anxious questions. "As a parent, believing I should know enough to protect my child, it is easy to rely on my imagination to reply to questions when there is no factual data on which to rely, but I can choose to let those questions go unanswered."

What Not to Worry About

To manage worry, it's important to know what not to worry about. Don't worry about what you can't control: "What if my child should contract a fatal disease?" Let go what you can't control and save your energy to invest in dealing with what you can. Don't equate worry with caring: "Well, if I didn't love you, I wouldn't worry about you so!" Driving yourself crazy with worry on behalf of your child is not an act of love; it is an act of fear. Don't invest worry with magical powers: "If I just worry hard enough about you, you'll be safe." Worry for superstition's sake provides no real protection. Don't let worry about now create more worries about the distant future: "If my child has this problem today, that means more troubles later on." Confine your worries to the present.

A Productive Use of Worry

Where parental worry comes in handy is in helping children learn to think ahead, anticipate possible problems, and prepare contingency plans should those problems arise. Young and adolescent children are often focused on getting what they want now: "I just want to be allowed to go to the mall and hang out with my friends!"

It is at this point that the conscientious parent begins to ask worry questions. "If you get separated from your friends, what will you do?" To the impatient fourteen-year-old, who anticipates only pleasure, this introduction of possible problems just gets in the way. "Oh, stop worrying, nothing bad is going to happen to me, just let me go!" But the parent is steadfast. "If you want me to consider giving you new freedoms, then you have to be willing to think through with me what risks you will be taking and how you will cope if any of those possibilities actually arise."

Even though worry can feel bad, it isn't necessarily bad. Even though it can be unrealistic, it can also be realistic. In fact, constructively used, parental worry can help train a child to think ahead, so in that sense, worry can do a lot of good.

ALERT!

Parents who constantly worry about what might happen to their son or daughter, and who communicate those worries to the child on a regular basis, may encourage him or her to become preoccupied by fears, overcautious with risk, and timid about trying something new.

The Importance of Rules

A child who grows up in an extremely chaotic, permissive, or neglectful family setting may not learn rule-following skills at home and, consequently, may be ill-prepared to fit into school. Continually reprimanded for not conforming to classroom procedures and following classroom rules, the child feels treated as "bad" when he or she is not—the child just wasn't prepared to get along in school.

A child who is highly indulged at home may also have a hard time adjusting to school because he is not used to being made to do what he doesn't like to do. "Why should I have to stop working on a project and go on to something else when I'm not finished?" An only child who may be used to receiving total attention from, and being given equal standing with, adults at home may have a hard time bending to adult authority at school. "The teacher just tells me to do what I'm told and won't always call on me when I know the answer!"

 **ESSENTIAL**

> If you have reason to believe rules at school may be very different from rules at home, then predict for your child what some of these differences are going to be. "At school you will be treated as one of many children, not like at home where you're the only one."

Children are typically ambivalent about family rules. On the one hand, rules prescribe certain behaviors and prohibit others, so rules limit personal freedom. On the other hand, rules decide how conduct will be regulated and how relationships will work, so rules provide family structure.

You should explain the necessity of having rules. "We create a family by making rules for all of us to safely and happily live by. So long as you depend on us to take care of you, you have to live on some of our terms. These terms often include following rules that we believe are part of learning to live responsibly. Some of these rules have reasons—like hygiene for health, like precautions for safety, like communication for keeping us adequately informed. Other rules are based on values—like how we believe you should treat other people, what kind of treatment you owe yourself, and how you should behave in public."

A Form of Security

All rules are limits ("You can't," "You must"), but not all limits are rules ("You only have so much money saved to spend"). Come adolescence, if not before, children often protest rules and the demands and restraints they impose. "You're too strict! You're over-protective!" To make matters worse, many situational rules apply double standards. As parents, you are exempt from many of the rules you make. So your child complains, "How come I have to have a bedtime and you don't? It's not fair!" Rules and those who make the rules are often resented.

On the other hand, rules create a predictable structure to live within, and that causes the child to feel secure. "I may not like all their rules, but at least I know what my parents expect of me." Having parents in charge of making rules lifts a lot of the burden of decision-making off the child. "I can't because my parents won't let me" is not just a complaint; it is often a relief. The child thinks, "That's one decision I don't have to figure out."

 **FACT**

Extreme obedience to parents can encourage a child to be too dependent on her parents. Because independent children are often less compliant, the price to pay for having independent children may be more resistance to parents at home.

Parents who are unstructured, inconsistent, or extremely permissive can give a child too many choices too early. For example, without sufficient rules to follow, an energetic four-year-old can become frantic with freedom, pushing his parents to exhaustion until, for their own sake and the child's, they finally impose a firm and reliable schedule. The predictability of the stricter system allows the child to settle down. To feel in control, your child needs to have sufficient parental controls (demands and limits) on which to depend. High-energy children who have a hard time paying attention, slowing down, and keeping still tend to need more structure from rules than more attentive children with less restless energy to manage.

Two Kinds of Rules

As the parents, your job is to make the rules that run the family. Generally speaking, you will be making two kinds of rules. You will make abiding rules that apply to everyone, to which no exceptions are made. Abiding rules are usually based on values. For example, "In this family, we do not steal from each other, we do not hit each other, and we do not call each other hurtful names." Abiding rules apply always and usually to everyone.

You will also make situational rules that may not apply to everyone. In addition, you may sometimes decide to make exceptions to situational rules. Situational rules deal with matters of management. For example, "In this family, everyone has weekend chores to do, children will do weeknight homework before they get to play, and on Sundays we will all get together with grandparents for supper." Situational rules apply most of the time.

Being Consistent

Abiding rules need to be consistently observed to support the values for which those rules stand: "The use of curse words in this home is simply not allowed." If you don't patrol the standard of family communication in which you believe, how children talk will not turn out to be how you want. "Now he swears at me when he gets angry!"

Situational rules should be consistently in place so long as they are relevant, but with room for intentional inconsistency when special circumstances or changing needs arise. Without this flexibility, you could find yourself trapped into a single rigid choice. "I said 8:00 P.M. is your bedtime, and I'm not going to bend that rule. You're just going to have to go to school without all your homework done." The observance of situational rules allows room for adjustments and exceptions. "Because you have so much homework tonight, I'm willing to let you stay up until 8:30 to get it done."

ESSENTIAL

It's important to be consistent about enforcing situational rules to let your child know you are serious about certain behaviors. For example, soon it will simply become a habit for your child to clean his bedroom every weekend, without being reminded.

Being Inconsistent

The kind of parental inconsistency that undermines situational rules is accidental inconsistency—where you're too tired, or too busy, or you forget to supervise. Accidental inconsistency tells your son or daughter that you don't really care about the rule, and it encourages children to ignore it, too. So you forget to supervise the room cleaning this weekend and your child "forgets" to do it the next weekend. Accidental exceptions undermine normal expectations.

On the other hand, intentional inconsistency can strengthen a situational rule—when you let the child know in advance that you choose to make an exception due to a special circumstance. Intentional inconsistency shows that this exception "proves the rule." "Normally you'd have to do your room next weekend, but because you'll be just getting back from your trip, you can wait a week." The intentional exception puts the child on notice that the following week, chores will be back to business as usual. Intentional exceptions reinforce normal expectations.

The Power of Prohibition

By midadolescence (ages thirteen to fifteen), your teenager knows that he or she is no longer living in the "age of command" where obedience to parents is unquestioned. Now the young person is living in the "age of consent," knowing full well that parental "control" depends on his or her willingness to comply.

What a liberating thought! "My parents can't actually make me do anything or stop me from doing anything! It's all up to me!" Far from just being exhilarating, however, this awareness of freedom is also frightening. "What's to stop me from going too far? Who's there to keep me from getting hurt?" The answer is, "Only myself!"

Even at this age of self-acknowledged independence from parental control, your midadolescent will sometimes depend on parental prohibition as a protection. If your daughter doesn't want to go along with something her friends have suggested, but doesn't want to risk making a refusal that could damage her social standing, she will appreciate being able to fall back on your rules about what she can and can't do. She may even "blame" you and your rule. "My parents won't let me. They never let me do anything."

Come adolescence, you want significant prohibitions clearly in place so your child can call on them for protection should the need arise. Prohibitions provide a value reference, a rule to follow, and an excuse your child can use to save face by blaming her parents for her refusal so she doesn't have to take responsibility for refusing herself.

Even if your child is going through a rebellious period, you need to hold fast to your prohibitions, giving your teenager the constant opportunity to sometimes reluctantly (but secretly gratefully) consent to living on your disciplinary terms.

 **FACT**

Rebellion against parental rules does not mean those rules are not working. It means those rules are being tested by the child to gather growing power of resistance to see if those rules can be changed, or to see if parents will really stand by what they say.

Outside Influences

No matter your family rules, no matter your family values, by age two or three, outside societal influences—which you may or may not approve of—will become part of your child's life. Friends, TV, movies, the Internet, magazines, popular music, video games, toys, and advertising all exercise enormous cultural influence on your child.

Some of that influence will be inconsistent with your rules and values and the discipline you want your child to learn. Your child will be confronted with:

- Alluring images and messages you wish your child didn't see and hear.
- Value positions that contradict what you are trying to teach.
- Popular ways of believing and behaving that your child admires and you do not.
- Marketing that tries to capture your child's attention and shape your child's taste.

There's no way to avoid it: These influences will find their way into your child's world. Like uninvited strangers, they will come into your home and arouse your child's curiosity and excite your child's interest. So what are you supposed to do?

First, you have to decide if there are some of these strangers you absolutely do not want to allow into your home—certain types of TV shows, video games, Internet content, movies, magazines, and music that you want to keep out.

But prohibition by itself has no educational value. What it usually provides is delay until the child is older. This is why, for example, some parents strike a bargain with a child wanting to watch an R-rated movie because friends have already seen it. "You can watch it at home with us on the condition that afterward we all discuss the examples the movie sets and the messages it sends." Parents want to weigh in with their approach to this material to give the child some mature guidelines for evaluating the adult content that he's seeing in the movie.

Internet Overexposure

Because the Internet opens up a world of information and online interaction for a child, you have to decide where in this infinite world of life exposure you want and do not want your child to go. Web sites that parents typically want their child to avoid include those trafficking in pornographic sex, recreational drug use, criminal violence, extreme physical risk-taking, credit card gambling, and intergroup hate.

Being curious and attracted to the forbidden, and left unsupervised with a world of temptation at their fingertips, your children may seek out or accidentally discover Internet sites they have been told to avoid. Now what?

Even if you restrict access after the fact, the information remains in the child's head. At this point, angry at disobedience and frightened by the unwelcome influence, your immediate response as a parent may be to come down hard with punishment to let your child know he or she has done wrong. As the first response, this is a mistake because your anger and sanctions only shut down the child's willingness to communicate about what happened.

ESSENTIAL

If you plan to protect your child from certain things by prohibiting them, you should also start thinking about what kind of preparation you want to give your child for when he or she encounters that experience later on.

When your child has seen an Internet site you don't want him to, you need to immediately turn the experience into a talking point to discuss what he saw, what he thought, and what he learned. Discovering how your child interpreted the experience—was he appalled? was he fascinated? did it scare him?—allows you to assess the effect and determine what you might say to influence the ideas your child carried away from the experience. To help draw this information out of your child, who is reluctant to talk after being caught, proceed with curiosity, not condemnation. "Although I would wish you hadn't seen this site, since you have, I'd like to know what you think of it. Tell me five things you think it is trying to communicate." Then use the answer as the basis for discussion.

Now you can weigh in with an alternative way to evaluate and frame the child's Internet experience. And then you can also make a family policy decision: "The Internet is filled with these kinds of pictures, but for the good of our family, we don't want them coming into our home."

Sometimes, a child will feel inclined to act out what he or she has seen on the Internet. At this point, you need to intervene. Seeing does not justify doing. You do not want what the child has seen to translate into what the child does. Suppose, for example, your daughter has accidentally visited a hate site. After you have discovered what she thought of it, and after you have responded with a perspective of your own, you may need to take a disciplinary stand against the use of harmful beliefs and hateful language if your child starts expressing them. "We don't want you spreading those beliefs or using that language because we believe that is wrong to do." Give the reasons that cause you to believe it is wrong as well.

One final and obvious instruction for your child about the Internet is to never give any personal information such as name, address, or phone number to anyone with whom he or she is interacting.

Prohibition Plus Preparation

By itself, prohibition has no educational value. It just fosters ignorance, often increasing the allure of what's forbidden. In addition, once children enter adolescence, curiosity about the larger world dramatically increases, the forbidden side of life becoming even more tempting to discover. Therefore, if you are going to prohibit your child from something, it is very important to fully explain your reasons for doing so, respecting his or her objections, listening when you disagree, learning from this disagreement more about your child's changing interests and point of view.

In addition, remember that your prohibition can affect your

child's standing with friends. When you prohibit things that your child's friends are allowed, you are asking your child to pay a personal and social cost. It's not just that your child wanted to see that movie, it's that now all her friends will share that experience and knowledge and she will not. "I really feel out of it! Everyone knows the story except me!" She may feel she has less in common with her friends, making her feel less like she belongs. The more out of the cultural loop she becomes, the more important gaining acceptance from peers may seem to her.

 **QUESTION?**

How can parents respond to the common complaint, "I'm the only one of my friends not allowed to go"?
Parents can reply, "We will help create another way for you to be with your friends."

Giving Your Opinion

When outside influences you are concerned about have entered your child's life, listen to your child's impression of what was seen or heard, and then communicate your own point of view. For example, you may decide to editorialize on entertainment that your child may unquestioningly accept. "I know that movie makes it sound normal and exciting for young people to drive fast and recklessly, but I want you to know that that endangers people's lives, and I never want you to do that when you get old enough to drive."

Or with an older adolescent who is already beginning to hear stories from peers about adventures with substance abuse, you decide to weigh in with a different perspective. "I know you're laughing—as the writers of the TV show intended you to—because the drunk person fell down at a party and upended a table of food on other people. But I'd like you to know that although in one way that looked funny, in another way it was not. If that drunk person was me and you were there, would you be laughing at what happened, or might you feel embarrassed that I had lost control of myself in a public situation? And how would you like cleaning up the mess I had made? For me, getting drunk is not as funny as it seems."

By giving your opinion, some bad examples that are communicated through the media can be used as the basis for some good instruction. You cannot alter your child's thinking, but you can definitely express your more mature, adult perspective. And you should. "We're not trying to change your mind. What you believe is for you to decide. We just want to give you an additional way to think about what you just saw." Use your experience and values as a filter through which to help interpret unwelcome outside influences that enter your child's world.

CHAPTER 9

Raising Responsible Children

I F YOU HAD TO HAVE ONLY ONE GOAL of discipline, raising responsible children would be a good one to choose. Why? Because your child needs both responsible behavior and responsibility to chart a steady course to independence. Both attributes allow the child to grow in strong and healthy ways.

Two Elements

If a responsible child is one who has been taught responsible behavior and responsibility, how are you going to help your child develop both of these attributes? To begin with, you need to be very clear about the difference between the two. They are not the same.

What's the Difference?

Responsible behavior is governing one's conduct according to ethical standards one has learned: "My parents taught me that being thrifty means not wasting what I use." Responsibility is the capacity to own the consequences of one's decisions: "I got a speeding ticket because I wasn't watching how fast I was driving."

Teach responsible behavior by limiting freedom and prescribing choice. "To save electricity, turn off the lights when you leave a room." Teach responsibility by giving freedom and permitting choice. "How you drive is now up to you, as is coping with the consequences of whatever driving choices you make." Parents teach responsible behavior by holding on, and teach responsibility by letting go.

In general, parents find it easier to teach responsible behavior than responsibility because teaching responsible behavior lets them feel more in control of what is going on.

Why Learning Both Matters

Don't automatically assume that because your child has learned one that he or she has necessarily learned the other.

For example, a well-behaved child is not necessarily a child who has learned responsibility. Raised in strict obedience to stern parental authority "or else," a child may have learned the rules of responsible conduct that his parents taught him, but he has never been given sufficient freedom of choice to learn to own the consequences of independent choice, having always done only what he was told to do.

 **ESSENTIAL**

Practice socially inclusive parenting. Don't send children away when adult company arrives or seat them at separate tables when it's time to eat. Instead, let them join in conversation with grownups and they will develop more responsible, grown-up social skills.

Or consider a child who has learned enormous power of responsibility but may never have been taught any rules for responsible behavior. Neglected by parents too preoccupied to care, the child is given great freedom to learn from natural consequences of choices made but is uninstructed about what constitutes responsible behavior.

When you teach your child what constitutes responsible behavior, you implant a code of values he or she can follow that will favor doing what is right over doing what is wrong. When you teach your child responsibility, you are giving him or her the mechanism for learning from experience, and for making better choices by considering the likely consequences.

Teaching Responsible Behavior

Every family defines what constitutes responsible behavior differently, depending on the values the parents hold. However, it is taught the same way in every family—by example and instruction.

Teaching the Preverbal Child

With a child too young to be instructed verbally, you must show how you want things done by using yourself as an example. Consider teaching a two-year-old "responsible" eating behavior. You want her to learn to use a spoon, not just her hands. So, as much as possible, you make it an imitation game. First, you put the spoon of food in your mouth and smile. Then the little child attempts to do the same and laughs with delight as this game of imitation builds between you. As the repetition goes on, your little child learns something serious from play. Don't punish undesirable behavior; interrupt it instead. If she throws down the spoon and tries to scoop up food in her hand, redirect her attention with some other activity or toy. Then try the eating-with-the-spoon game again, rewarding desirable behavior with a smile and a cheer when it occurs.

 **FACT**

Though parents often begin by using mostly positive responses to shape a young child's behavior, they typically resort to more negative responses as the child grows older. But rewarding the positive works better than punishing the negative, no matter the child's age.

Dressing oneself, hygiene, picking up and cleaning up and putting back are all taught in the same way with the preverbal child.

You keep instruction light and playful; you make it a game. And you use very little negative correction, and then only of the most gentle kind.

When the child hits you in the face because she feels angry at being put to bed, clasp the child's hands, look the child in the eyes, and seriously (not angrily) repeat the word "No" while shaking your head. Then you hug her and smile and put her down. If she hits you again in anger, repeat the corrective process because, as an adult, you understand that children do not learn from just one episode of instruction. Over time she will come to understand that the headshake "No" means that you don't want her to repeat what she just did.

Obviously, you do not want to hit a child for hitting, or yell at a child to stop yelling, because that only teaches by example the behavior you wish to stop.

A Model for Teaching Responsible Behavior

One way for parents to organize their instruction of responsible behavior is around the concept of care. Think about a four-part curriculum that you want to teach. Some suggested topics are included in each part to get you started adding more.

- **Caring for self:** maintaining one's own health and hygiene, care of space and possessions, cleaning up and picking up after oneself, providing for and protecting oneself.
- **Caring for family others:** showing consideration, sharing what one has, helping others out, being supportive in hard times.
- **Caring for the family unit:** contributing to chores and services, compromising for the larger good, communicating about common concerns.
- **Caring for outside others:** respecting rights of others, obeying social rules, concern for human welfare, volunteering community help.

Coming up with categories of responsible behavior is the first step. Second is specifying the actions that will put those categories into actual operation. And third is having the child repeat these actions often enough so that responsible behavior becomes a habit. So when it comes to caring for outside others, having practiced this on a regular basis in the family, it seems only natural to your child to spend some volunteer time each month helping others less fortunate than herself.

 **ESSENTIAL**

One way to reinforce the importance of responsible behaviors is to get your child involved with other people—good friends, extended family, or church, for example—who practice your values of responsible conduct.

Supporting Family Needs

A final way you teach your child responsible behavior is to depend on him or her to help fulfill family needs. The message is, "To function as a family we need your participation, contribution, and help." For the family to function well as a whole, each member must take some share in its support. Children who are expected to perform some useful tasks to support the family not only develop self-esteem from being valued for the service they provide, but they also become more invested in family itself because of the contribution they have made.

The family that invests in family is one in which a host of responsible behaviors are taught by doing many things together. Such a family may talk together, problem solve together, do household chores together, do family projects together, play together, go to worship together, prepare special occasions together, and pull together in mutual support in times of crisis. Responsible behavior shared by everyone forms the core of a healthy family life.

Teaching Responsibility

Responsibility is one of the hardest skills for parents to teach. The decisions about when to let go and what decisions to turn over to the child can be complicated. Teaching responsibility is scary for parents to do since it requires turning over some freedom of choice to their son or daughter, who is now at risk from consequences of his or her own independent decision-making.

Let go too early, and the child may be at risk of immature judgment. For example, excited and overconfident from learning to balance on a bike, believing that is all there is to riding, the child takes off down the street, gathers speed, and crashes into a parked car because steering is not yet under control. The parents let go too soon. More preparation was required. At worst, too much parental letting go creates permissiveness that offers no protection for the child.

ALERT!

Since responsibility requires taking risks as your child tries to handle a new freedom on his own, first determine what kind of risk-taker your child is—very bold or very cautious. You may have to restrain the bold child with caution and embolden the cautious child with encouragement.

Let go too late, and the child can be at risk of inexperienced decision-making. For example, by waiting until the late adolescent is older before teaching how to manage credit, the young person blithely overcharges a credit card in college and gets into serious debt. The parents held on, held back, and put off an important experience too long. That's the problem with protection—it offers no preparation.

Steps in Turning over Responsibility

Teaching responsibility in a responsible fashion is labor intensive.

1. You show the child how to do something by explanation and demonstration.
2. You help the child to do it with your advice and support.
3. You monitor how the child does it with supervision.
4. You let the child practice it on his or her own within limits suitable for a beginner.
5. You turn over responsibility by letting go, letting the child do it independently.
6. You hold the child accountable for good and bad consequences, reviewing the lessons that both kinds of consequences have to teach.

Deciding What Freedoms to Turn over and When

There are two visions of what are appropriate responsibilities for a child to learn—the parent's and the child's. Often the child considers the responsibilities she wants to be desirable freedoms of self-determination, and yet considers the responsibilities parents want her to have as unfair burdens of work.

At the age of six, your daughter may believe she should have freedom to decide what she wants to eat. At the age of ten, she may believe she should have freedom to decide what she watches on TV. At the age of twelve, she may believe she should have freedom to decide whether or not to do homework. "I'm responsible enough to make my own choices!" The problem is, however, none of these are freedoms her parents are willing to turn over, because although the child isn't bothered by the consequences of inadequate diet, televised sex and violence, and school failure, her parents definitely are.

What you can propose are other freedoms that you want the child to responsibly assume. At age six, you want your child to take responsibility for keeping track of personal belongings so you don't have to keep checking. At age ten, your child should be taking responsibility for cleaning up after and feeding the dog so you don't have to keep reminding. At age twelve, your child should be ready for the responsibility of keeping his or her bedroom clean so you don't have to keep nagging. Yet none of these responsibilities holds much allure for your child.

So to begin with, parents have to decide what freedoms they are willing to turn over, at what age, in order to create the opportunity for learning what responsibilities.

As an exercise, to get started thinking about when you would want your child to learn different areas of responsibility, order the following list of responsibilities from what you would be inclined to let go first to what you would be inclined to let go last.

_____ Choosing what to eat

_____ Choosing when to go to bed

_____ Choosing what to watch on TV

_____ Choosing where to surf on the Internet

_____ Choosing what to wear to school

_____ Choosing when to start homework

_____ Choosing how to spend money

_____ Choosing whom to have as friends

_____ Choosing how often to bathe

_____ Choosing how to care for possessions

_____ Choosing how long to talk on the phone

There is no "right" or "wrong" for which of these areas of choice to let go of first or last in order to teach responsibility; but it is definitely your responsibility to come up with an order that fits your parenting values and objectives.

ALERT!

Don't turn over any freedom where you are unwilling to let your child learn from what bad consequences from bad choices would have to teach.

Separating Responsibility as Childhood Ends

A child usually enters early adolescence somewhere between the ages of nine and thirteen as he or she becomes more discontented with being defined and treated as a "child." Participating in older-age activities and experiencing the larger world outside of family now become more important as the young person begins to push against and pull away from parents for more freedom to grow.

From this critical growth point onward, the great protector for the child is going to be the power of responsibility the boy or girl possesses to make mindful and unimpulsive decisions as he or she experiments with new and different experiences. To safeguard their early adolescent, parents need to begin turning over three kinds of self-management responsibilities—for facing consequences of bad decisions, for recovering from unhappiness, and for solving problems.

Now that he's an adolescent and is pushing for more independence, parents need to be sure he is given the chance to learn more self-management responsibility. So, rather than rescue the child from the consequences of a bad decision, parents should help the early adolescent to take more responsibility for dealing with the outcomes of his or her actions. "We think you need to pay for what you did." Rather than provide some fix for the child's unhappiness, parents should enable the early adolescent to take more responsibility for recovering his or her own emotional well-being. "We want you to develop ways to cheer yourself back up when you are feeling down." And rather than jumping in and solving the child's problems, parents should encourage the early adolescent to take more responsibility for figuring out his or her own problems. "We want you to think out some possible solutions before we add any of our own." This is not to say that in all three cases parents totally back out of the early adolescent's life, only that they start doing more letting go than they did before.

Teaching Two-Step Thinking

One way of looking at teaching your child responsibility is as a process through which you help the boy or girl develop the habit of thinking twice. You want to teach your child to rely on second thought. This means helping your child learn the discipline of two-step thinking.

Consider child raising this way. When an infant is born into your care, he or she is a one-step or first-step thinker. What is this first step? It is the infant's knowing what he or she wants. Immediate gratification of wants is the infant's ruling impulse. As parents, you appreciate the importance of wants and urgency of impulse, but you know that a life governed only by wants and impulse will become destructive. This is why your job is, through discipline (instruction and correction), to train the growing boy or girl over time to become a two-step thinker.

 **ALERT!**

> Two-step thinking needs to be taught twice—first in childhood to help the child outgrow the tyranny of impulse that rules infancy, and then again with the onset of adolescence, when the urge to satisfy immediate wants returns.

What is the second step? The second step of two-step thinking is exercising judgment. You train the child to delay impulsively gratifying wants long enough so he or she can consider what is wise. You do this by reminding the child to think about consequences. "What happened before when you made this kind of choice? What might happen later if you make this kind of choice?" So when you see your child tempted to rush into a risky decision, you say, "Think twice about what you are going to do." And the child is reminded to delay wants long enough to exercise judgment by considering past and possible consequences. "On second thought, maybe I'll wait until tomorrow to decide what to say to my friend about our fight at school today. I'm feeling pretty hurt and angry right now." So what feels good at the moment is delayed until she can determine what is really the best thing to do.

The child takes time to think ahead. Present choice is being informed by predicting possible outcome. As want (telling the friend off) is influenced by judgment (taking time to cool down before speaking), your child is learning responsibility.

Readiness for Responsibility

How do you tell when it is wise to risk giving your child more freedom from which to learn more responsibility? What follows is a checklist of behaviors that you may want in place before you do more letting go.

- *Does the child self-correct from mistakes?* If bad experience informs better choices, this shows that lessons from erring can be learned. "Because of what happened, I won't do it again."
- *Does the child meet commitments?* If the child keeps promises and agreements, this shows that the child's word can be trusted. "I did what I said I would."
- *Does the child cooperate when requested to?* If the child helps when asked, this shows willingness to honor the needs of others. "I'll give you a hand."
- *Does the child complete plans that are started?* If the child finishes what is begun, this shows a determination to see intentions through. "I got things done just like I said I would."
- *Does the child consistently keep up activities that sustain well-being?* If the child maintains this continuity of effort, this shows dedication to what personally matters. "I practice so I can keep getting better."
- *Does the child comply with rules at home, at school, and out in the world?* If the child respects rules, this shows a willingness to fit in and go along with social restraints. "I stay out of trouble."
- *Is the child conscientious?* If the child keeps up with what you consider important without having to be told, this shows responsibility has been accepted. "I take care of what I am supposed to do on my own."

Children who at the present time generally don't meet these criteria are not ready to be given more responsibility. For parents, this means there is more training work to do.

The Choice/Consequence Connection

Begin with what seems obvious. Life is a chain of choice and consequence. As adults, you know that a lot of what happens to you is a consequence of decisions you make. Children, however, have to learn this connection. They have to learn that all choices have consequences. They have to learn to use past consequences to inform better choices the next time. They have to learn to make constructive choices now by anticipating future consequences. They have to learn that, to some degree, they can influence the consequences they get by the choices they make.

"I want to go outside and play," says the child.

"I want you to be able to go out and play, too," agrees the parent. "But what do you need to do first before you get to go outside?"

"Pick up my clothes," answers the child.

"That's right," congratulates the parent. "You can choose to pick up your clothes so you can get to go outside and play."

Sometimes the choice/consequence connection can be hard to learn because children tend to be shortsighted. They focus on what they want now, not considering how choices now can cost them later. So the child spends his three dollars at the corner convenience store this morning on an impulse buy, forgetting that he was going to save it for admission to a movie this afternoon. Why didn't he save his money? Because he was thinking only about his choice now, not connecting it with a later consequence.

So now he comes to his parents needing more money for the later spending he forgot he wanted to do. To help him understand the choice/consequence connection, they don't lecture or criticize. They just refuse the emergency financing he has requested, explaining, "Before spending your money, next time you may want to think ahead. Choices now can affect choices later on."

Who's Got the Problem?

As parents, you have to sometimes resist the temptation to protect your child from the consequences of his or her bad decisions. If you keep interceding between your child's choices and the bad consequences they create, then the problem that was originally your child's will become your own, your child will learn no lesson from the consequences he or she chose to create, and the same bad choices are more likely to continue. You have to let your child have the problem, and resist the temptation to take it over.

 **FACT**

> When parents pay for their child's consequences to protect their son or daughter from hurt, they usually buy the child's problem for themselves at their own and their child's expense. They prevent the child from learning more responsibility.

So parents complain about their first grader who, despite their reminders to bring them safely in, leaves new toys outside overnight. But then, after the child is in bed, the parents go and bring in the toys because they don't want their daughter to be victimized by theft and to suffer the consequence of loss and disappointment that would follow. Unfortunately, by sparing her this unhappy consequence, they are also keeping her from learning the responsibility that goes with taking care of her toys.

One of the hardest parts of parenting is letting your child face the consequences of his or her bad choices, learning from whatever hard lessons the choice/consequence connection has to teach. If the anticipated consequence would compromise the child's safety (teasing a neighbor's dog that might snap back) they need to explicitly state why the child must refrain from this behavior due to real risks of injury involved.

Natural Consequences

When a child experiences natural consequences from poor choices that he or she regrets, parents do not need to add correctional consequences of their own to teach a lesson. Instead, they can support the child with sympathy and explore what the unwanted consequence has to teach. So when your daughter neglected to bring in her newest toy at the end of the day as reminded, she found it missing the next morning. She's crushed and wants to know if you will replace it. No, you tell her, gone is gone. But you can express sympathy that it happened, then ask what she's learned from the loss. "Not to leave my toys outside overnight," she sadly concludes. Unhappily for all concerned, when parental words fail to instruct, hard experience often becomes the best teacher—if parents do not act to prevent the lesson from being taught.

Outside Social Consequences

In the same way, when a second grader is given lunchtime detention for a repeated classroom offense, and so misses out on socializing with friends, parents do need not to apply consequences for that classroom misbehavior at home. The school has given a consequence of its own. All you need to do as a parent is help the child see the connection between how she chose to act and how the school chose to respond. "We're sorry you missed lunch with your friends. How can you manage to behave in class so this doesn't happen to you again?"

 **ESSENTIAL**

Before applying any negative consequence for their child's misbehavior or mistake, parents need to ask themselves, "Has any natural or other social consequence occurred that will discourage this choice from being made again?" If so, don't pile on other consequences.

Casting off Responsibility

One helpful guideline to follow when teaching your child responsibility is "no accidents allowed." Don't let your child attempt to cast off responsibility for his actions by claiming something was an accident. Instead, help him to see how his actions led to that end result.

"It was an accident!" protests the child about how papers in the trash caught fire. "I didn't mean to set a fire. I thought the match was out." But lack of intent does not excuse the child from responsibility. So parents hold the child to account. "If you hadn't been lighting matches, there would have been no opportunity for the trash to catch fire." The child may well be innocent of intent, but the child is guilty of unthinking (and, in this case, forbidden) actions leading to an unacceptable outcome. "This is why we have a rule against your playing with matches. To prevent accidents."

 **FACT**

> The less a child values herself, the less responsibility for mistakes and misbehavior she is likely to accept, because she feels so inadequate already. Children who claim it is never their fault when it actually is, are often troubled by low self-esteem.

Another helpful guideline is "no blame allowed." Blame is the easy way out of responsibility. "The test was unfair; that's why I did so badly. It's the teacher's fault. Most of the questions were about things I didn't know she'd ask!" The problem with blame is that if the child believes that he wasn't at all at fault for something that happened and there wasn't anything he could have done differently, then the child is a helpless victim. Accepting some degree of responsibility empowers the child with choice to influence whether whatever happened will happen again. So parents work with the child to figure out if there was anything he or she could have done differently in preparation for the test to have done better on it. "Well, I could have answered the questions in the textbook, but who wants to do that?" Reply the parents, "Maybe you do now."

Counting Systems

Two time-honored training techniques of parents, in use probably since parenting began, have been systems of counting (toward consequence) and earning (rewards). Both techniques stand parents in good stead until the child enters adolescence, when they tend to become less influential and four other discipline factors (see Chapters 10 through 13) become more effective. Both systems teach the child to connect choice with consequence.

Counting systems tend to be based on avoiding negative consequences. "Look at me. I want you to know I am serious. I asked you to stop doing that. I've told you what will happen if you don't stop doing that. Now I'm going to count to three. 'One' is to give you warning. 'Two' is to let you know I mean business. And 'three' means I'm going to do what I said. One, two . . . Thank you for doing what I asked."

 **ESSENTIAL**

Some parents, with a low tolerance for frustration, use another age-old counting strategy to keep from losing their temper with a recalcitrant child. Counting to ten can help them cool down and maintain self-control to prevent overreaction.

What counting does is put the child on notice about how a choice now will soon lead to an unwanted consequence. Counting gives the child time to think. Does the child really want to pay the consequence for continuing to do what he or she has been asked to stop? The choice is up to the child, and the parent formally acknowledges that choice. Now the child knows, "I affect what my parent will do based on the choice I make."

Counting systems give warning. They focus attention on what the parent wants, they recognize the child's power of choice, they promise what will happen if compliance is not given, and they deliver the consequence as promised if compliance is refused.

Earning Systems

Earning systems tend to be based on gaining positive consequences. "I have posted a list of five things I want you to do every weekday to help me at home. At the end of each week we will check off which ones you have done. For twenty-five checks, you get to pick out a movie to rent to watch this weekend. For twenty to twenty-four checks, you get to pick out a favorite meal this weekend. For fifteen to nineteen checks, you get to go out and get ice cream this weekend." The weekend has become reward time for working hard all week.

With earning systems, a child attaches choices made now with gaining something special later. In addition, the posted list of "five things" serves as a daily reminder for the child about what parents want him or her to regularly do for them. What makes earning systems work is making sure the rewards being offered are ones that the individual child values, and that rewards earned are promptly and faithfully provided. So the first step in setting up the system is sitting with the child and coming up with a list of rewards that he or she would really value earning, special things not usually provided. Of course, few rewards have lasting interest, so parents and child have to keep altering the earning system to keep rewards appealing.

These systems can help your child learn responsibility as well as responsible behaviors, which will result in your goal of raising a responsible child.

CHAPTER 10

Guidance: The First Factor

THE FIRST FACTOR IN EFFECTIVE DISCIPLINE is guidance. Guidance is communication of a largely one-sided kind. It's the parent's asking, "What do I want my child to know from me?" The purpose of your guidance is providing information to help guide him or her through the process of growing up.

Good Parents Never Shut Up

There are many sources of information in the world out to influence your child's mind, but there are none to compete with you. It's not because you know so much, but because you care so much and your opinion matters so much. You have the child's best interests at heart because you are connected by love to the child, a claim that other sources of information cannot make. And that child, even in the disaffected teenage years, is by love connected to you. Knowing this, your child credits what you have to share so long as you are willing to speak up and have your say in a caring and respectful way.

The principle of guidance is really pretty simple. If there is something major or minor, good or ill, for certain or suspected, welcome or unwelcome, that you think your child could benefit from knowing, out of concern (not criticism): *Tell your child.*

Why Children Value Parental Guidance

Children want to know what their parents desire, think, believe, and value in order to have a reference to direct their own behavior. In childhood, the boy or girl often follows his or her parents' guidance in an attempt to be like them and to be liked by them. Similarity to parents not only feels rewarding but is usually rewarded with their approval. In adolescence, the young person, to some degree, may rebel against their guidance to assert more power by showing his or her opposition. In either case, however, the child is defining himself in relation to what his parents stand for—going along with or against what they value.

 **ESSENTIAL**

> Giving your child constant, honest, and respectful feedback about how she's conducting her life, and emphasizing what behavior you expect, lets your child always know exactly where she stands with you.

Parental guidance is like a compass. It allows children to chart their course based on a sense of direction they can trust. This is why, despite a child's disagreement or an adolescent's rebellion, parents need to keep their guidance coming. Give it up, and children and adolescents will seek the guidance they need elsewhere, from less reliable and loving sources, turning to peers and the popular culture to fill the void. Deprived of this parental compass, children flounder for direction and risk coming to harm, because bad advice from any source feels better than no advice at all.

Never Underestimate a Child's Ignorance

Think about what it's like to be your child. There's so much he or she doesn't know. There is so much ignorance about oneself and the world. All the way through growing up, there are so many unasked questions that need answers. "Where am I going?" "How am I doing?" "What should I believe?" "Which choice should

I make?" "Why is this happening?" "When am I going to be told?" "Who can I trust?" "Whose opinion is correct?"

All the way from early childhood to the end of adolescence, it is your job to continually speak to the changing content that these questions seek to reveal. Good parents never shut up, because good children constantly need to be told by a loving, wiser, mature adult how to sort out the perplexities of life, what to believe, and how to behave.

If you are reluctant to discharge this part of your responsibility, just consider the costs if you don't. For example, suppose one night at supper, your middle school child mentions that some kids were caught at school sniffing inhalants in the bathroom. Because you are not comfortable talking about drugs with your child, you just let the comment slide. What a mistake! Don't you understand that when your child mentions drugs and drug use at home, he or she is already getting lots of information about these subjects from friends? Do you want to weigh in with mature judgment and reliable information, or do you want to leave your child at the mercy of the immature judgment and unreliable information of ignorant peers who are excited by the forbidden? "Sniffing glue can't hurt you," friends (ignorant of brain damage these chemicals can cause) have assured your adolescent. "Huffing is fun. And it doesn't cost you. You can get off on all kinds of crazy stuff your parents keep around the house." Good parents never shut up.

 **ALERT!**

Just because your child doesn't want to talk to you is no good reason not to talk to your child. In fact, it's all the *more* reason to talk to your child.

The Power of Persuasion

For parents who are fearless and relentless and respectful communicators, guidance provides most of the disciplinary influence they ever need. They are fearless because they do not shy away from talking about anything the child wants to discuss or from pursuing important topics that the child is reluctant to talk about. They do not tiptoe around uncomfortable topics. They are relentless because they keep after an issue until it is fully addressed or finally resolved. They do not give up when the talking gets tough. And they are respectful because they listen to, and take seriously, whatever the child has to say, encouraging the child to do the same with them. They do not tune the child out or interrupt when they do not agree.

Advice That Sticks

Most parental persuasion does not come from arguing with your child, winning the argument, and changing your child's mind. It doesn't come from controlling your child's choice of how to think and what to decide. Your ability to persuade comes from informing the child's choice by offering a piece of advice or a point of view that the child is willing to consider. "Just for your information, this is what I think about what you told me and why. And this is what I think is in your best interests to do about the situation."

 **ESSENTIAL**

> When you and your child see an issue differently, you have much more influence discussing to create understanding than you do by arguing in order to win.

The role of guidance is to offer an additional value reference to the mix of beliefs created by the child's personal views, the child's peers, and the popular culture he encounters every day. A parent's job is not to change the child's mind, but to offer a responsible alternative frame of reference on an ongoing basis.

For example, peers may be telling your child how funny it is to egg the front door of someone they don't like. As parents, you may disagree. "How you think about this is up to you, but just for the record, I see it a different way. I think when people deliberately deface other people's property, they are doing injury to those people and should have to pay for what they do." Don't argue with the child's opinion, because that will just strengthen the opposition between you. Your input is more powerful than your argument. "You have a right to your opinion. I just want you to know, I don't see it that way."

Input respects the child's power of choice, and shows him that you respect him, which means he is more apt to listen to and consider what you have to say. Argument creates a power struggle, where winning (or not losing) becomes more important than gaining understanding. You want to influence how your child understands life, not to domineer your child's thinking. Parents can't control the child's choice, but they can inform the child's choice.

Giving Good Information

The most effective parents are not high controllers; they are good informers. Some hallmarks of a good informer are:

- Willingness to offer alternative opinions, while not insisting on being right.
- Willingness to listen openly to opposing opinions, not with your mind shut down because it is already made up.
- Willingness to discuss differing opinions in order to increase mutual understanding, not turning a difference into an argument you feel you have to win.
- Willingness to be educated by what the other person has to say.

Parents don't have to have all the answers. Parents don't have to know what to do about every situation that troubles the child's life. A lot of times the best a parent can offer is, "I'll help you think the problem through, and maybe together we can come up with a solution or plan that will answer your need."

Ironically, the power of parental persuasion begins by declaring to the child, "What to think and how to act are ultimately up to you." The power of parent as wise counselor is offering, not ordering. Children who have this parent resource are usually very grateful for it. "I can talk to my mom about anything, and I can always trust her to tell me what she honestly thinks."

Partnering with Your Child

As a parent, you are guiding your child along his or her path in life. You do this partly by being older and more experienced, having trod the path of childhood before, and you do it partly in consultation with your child, who informs you about the changed realities of growing up today.

In a way, what you are doing is forming a partnership with your child. This partnership is between a generalist and a specialist, trying to combine the understandings of both to serve the growing needs of your son or daughter.

The Parent as Generalist

You are the generalist. Because you have lived longer, have more experience, and have extensive exposure to the larger world, you have some general understandings about life that your child lacks. Thus, although your seventh grader may not see the importance of working hard in school, you paid a price for achieving poorly that you wish to spare your temporarily disaffected son or daughter. This is why you keep after your child to see that homework gets done.

The Child as Specialist

Your child is the specialist. No one understands her self and her social world better than she does. And she is familiar with the peer culture in which she lives in ways you will never be. Thus, although the music she listens to may sound strident and abrasive to your ears, it inspires her with popular anthems about the emotional trials of growing up and the longing for independence. This is why she insists on blaring her music to keep her company when she is doing the homework that she doesn't like to do. She needs the distraction of what she likes to help her concentrate on what she doesn't like. The partnership has reached a compromise. You each know what is in her best interests. The generalist supports doing the work. The specialist knows how to make doing the work bearable.

ALERT!

If you can't listen and learn from your child's special knowledge, it is unlikely your child will be able to listen and learn from your general understanding. Your persuasive power is partly dependent on your being open to being enlightened by your child.

Guidance is often a two-way street. When it comes to charting a healthy course for your child's life, two heads can be better than one. There's a lot your child doesn't know, but there's also a lot you don't know. Never forget that the best informant about the realities of your child's world is your child. Parents who tell their child to "shut up" have just shut themselves off from learning about their child.

Giving Feedback about Performance

Since your child is constantly performing (from doing chores at home, to complying with rules in society, to doing classroom work at school), you have a role in monitoring your child's performance and giving a continuing stream of feedback about how he or she is doing.

As you already know, focusing on positive performance is much more productive than becoming preoccupied with the negative. Noticing and recognizing how your son or daughter continues to get up in time for school, once again has remembered to write down all assignments, and keeps doing homework without being asked, all support continuation of behaviors you want your child to practice.

The fact that today the child had a fight with another child in the lunch line over who got there first (and got sent to the office for it) should not be treated as the only indicator of how the child is doing at school. It should be discussed, but within the larger context that this was unusual conduct and not the norm. In addition, consequences imposed by the school should suffice. Outside of discussion, parents should impose no further sanctions.

 **FACT**

Performance feedback is your tool to show your child that you notice and appreciate good performance and do not focus just on the negative.

Using Grades to Grade Your Feedback Style

Suppose your child's report card showed two A's, three B's, and one C. Which of the following would likely be your first reaction?

- "I would first notice the C and want to know what's going wrong and talk about getting it fixed."
- "I would first notice the two A's and try to find out how the other grades could also be raised to A's."
- "I would notice that five of the six grades were B or above and congratulate my child for doing well."

The child who made these grades might have a different reaction to each of these responses. To the first response, the child might declare, "You just focus on the one bad grade and don't even notice the good ones!" To the second response, the child might declare, "No matter how well I do, you're never satisfied!" And to the third response, the child might declare, "You always help me feel good about my work at school!" Which kind of response would you like your child to make?

Evaluative and Descriptive Feedback

After your child has given a speech as part of a holiday PTA program at school, do you give evaluative or descriptive feedback?

Evaluative feedback would be something like, "Good for you, you did a great job!" From this, the child knows that parents have been generally pleased for the child, but he doesn't know specifically by what. This is why you need to give descriptive feedback as well. "The way you stood up straight, squared your shoulders, talked slowly and clearly and in a loud voice really made what you had to say effective." When your descriptive feedback itemizes specifics, your child not only feels deeply noticed, but can also identify some of the behaviors that contributed to doing a "great job."

Sharing about Yourself

Most of what parents have to give their children is information about who and how they are. Learning about one's parents teaches children about themselves. "In a lot of ways I'm like my dad." One reason adopted children seek out their biological parents is to claim important personal history in order to better understand themselves. An important part of giving guidance is allowing your children to come to know you, their guide. Both your personal history and your current experience with life have much to teach.

ALERT!

The way you treat your child teaches him how to treat himself. Continually criticize your child, and he learns to become self-critical. Constantly value your child, and he learns to become self-valuing.

Sharing Personal History

Consider how much guidance you can give by sharing information about your personal past. By sharing with your children bad decisions you made as a child ("I decided school wasn't worth the effort and dropped out"), you can help them learn from your mistakes.

You can also help them learn from good decisions that you made ("I was badly injured playing sports freshman year, but I didn't give up, I worked hard to rehabilitate, and sophomore year I was able to play again"). In this case, you give them a personal example of determination. There are powerful cautionary and inspiring stories to be told by sharing your personal history.

Sharing Current Experience

You also can provide guidance by sharing the experiences from your life now. Your child has a problem with temper when frustration goes on too long or gets too high at school, so you share your own experiences with managing frustration at work. You also share strategies you have developed to keep frustration from exploding into anger. "I've learned to shrink daily frustrations down to size by comparing them to really serious problems that I'm grateful I don't have. And if I feel myself moving toward anger, I've learned to change my mind and think of happy things instead. These techniques work for me. Maybe they could work for you."

Or you lose your job, and your household income drops. How can you use this experience to teach your child? "What's happened to me has an important lesson for you to understand. There's no lifetime employment. There's no permanent job. There's no secure occupation. That's how life is for me and how it will be for you. So I'm going to be talking to you about how I am going about looking for new work and how I keep my spirits up while I'm looking. We will all be learning to live on less money for a while until I find another job, so I will also be talking to you about that. Knowing how to sometimes make do with less is another skill you will need in life."

Children Learn from Other People's Lives

Why would parents withhold this information? Parents give many reasons. "Parents aren't supposed to talk with their child about their mistakes or problems." "My child wouldn't be interested." "I'm not comfortable talking about myself." "It's none of my child's business." "I don't want my child using information about my past as permission to repeat my mistakes."

Children are vicarious learners. They learn a lot about life by hearing about the lives of other people. Think of all they learn about life from the lives of friends. Thank goodness they can satisfy a lot of their curiosity about life without having to actually experience it. Hearing about something is enough. So, a friend of your fifth grader's, who is sneaking out after her parents are asleep, tells your child about the wild side of life to be seen late at night wandering a dangerous downtown. For lots of children, wild friends are valued as good informants but are also recognized as bad companions. Your child is certainly interested in hearing about these adventures, but he or she has no desire to follow along.

Like your child's friends, you, too, are a window on the world if you will allow yourself to be. So at the dinner table, you ask about your child's day and get only a minimal reply: "It was okay." You wish your child would tell you more, but further questions only get more minimal replies. No wonder he or she is not forthcoming. At the age of twelve, your early adolescent finds your questions intrusive. They invade privacy and are emblematic of authority, often resented and resisted on both counts.

 **ESSENTIAL**

Parents who will not disclose information about themselves usually train their child to be the same way. If you want your child to confide in you, then confide in your child—not for support, but for education.

So what can you do to encourage more open sharing? Talk about what your day was like, what went well and what went badly, how you felt when things went badly, and how you kept yourself going even so. You can't force your child to talk, but by talking about your own day in specific and emotional detail, you are opening up a window on your world through which your child can see more about life, and you are modeling sharing behavior you would like your child to follow.

The Power of a Good Talking-To

There's nothing worse for most children than being told at great and explicit length they have done wrong—when they already know they've done wrong and just want to forget it and move on. But the parent is resolved to wear the subject out. "You need to know that whenever you step out of line, I am going to have my say about it as long as I want to talk about it, and you are going to have to listen until I am done. Whatever else trouble gets you, it will always get you a good talking-to from me."

 **QUESTION?**

What does "positive criticism" sound like?
"I don't understand how someone who is usually so reliable could have forgotten to let me know. This isn't like you. You make such responsible decisions most of the time. You usually call me when you are going to be late, and I really appreciate it."

"Aren't you done lecturing yet?" asks the child who is weary from hearing his parent go on and on about how skipping out of school was wrong and why it shouldn't happen again. "Honey, I'm not even warmed up yet. And another thing I want you to think about is . . ." This unwelcome guidance will continue until the parent feels that all lessons to be learned from this unhappy episode have been taught.

Lecturing works. A good talking-to is a lecture, and most children hate having their parents "lecture" them on what was done wrong. "I said I was sorry, so you don't need to say any more." "No," replies the parent. "One consequence for what you did is hearing me out. I'll let you know when I'm done, and until I am done you will listen to what I have to say."

What is "good" about a lecture is that it starts negatively but ends positively. Begin by specifically describing the wrong that has occurred, then explain why it is wrong, explain how you feel in response, describe what has to happen differently so your child doesn't make this choice again, and then draw lessons that the child should learn. Finish with a strong statement of faith that you know your child knows better, and let him or her know that you understand that this violation is an exception and that, in most cases, he or she behaves very well. So you start with "negative criticism" and end with "positive criticism."

A reversal of the "good talking-to" that is very effective is requiring the errant child to do all the talking—describing what happened, why it happened, and why it won't happen again—for however long it takes the parent to feel the topic has been exhausted. "Can I stop talking about it now?" asks the weary child. "Not until I've heard enough," replies the parent.

When parents are committed to guidance as their primary disciplinary approach, the three other factors in effective discipline—supervision, punishment, and working the exchange points—are rarely called into play. Declaration and discussion provide discipline enough.

CHAPTER 11

Supervision: The Second Factor

THE SECOND BASIC TECHNIQUE of effective discipline is supervision. Supervision has two components—keeping after the child and keeping track of the child. Supervision is equal parts pursuit and surveillance.

Good Parents Never Give Up

Children dislike being kept after because it feels like they can't escape parental demands. "You already told me! You don't have to tell me again! I heard you the first time! Stop repeating what you said!" Replies the parent, "I will be glad to stop repeating what I said when you start doing what I asked."

"You're nagging!" the child accuses. "I hate it when you nag!" "So do I," agrees the parent. "It's the drudge work of parenting. It's irritating to you and it's exhausting for me. But if you keep putting off my request, I'll keep on nagging until I get it met."

Children dislike being kept track of because it limits their freedom and invades their privacy. "I hate how you keep checking up on me to see where I am and what I'm doing! Don't you trust me?" Replies the parent, "The more often I find out that you are where we agreed, the more I trust you." "You're spying!" accuses the child. "I hate it when you keep checking up on me!" "So do I," agrees the parent. "It's offensive to you and it's not fun for me, but part of my job is knowing where you are at all times."

Supervision needs to be done. It means being willing to back up your requests with repetition and being willing to confirm the whereabouts of your child with checking. Pursuit and surveillance, nagging and checking, are honorable work for which you will get no thanks. Thankless parenting—that's what supervision is.

Yet, though they complain that supervision is irritating and invasive, children can miss it when parents abandon this responsibility, because of what it symbolically represents. Without enough supervision, children may feel that you've given up on them. Your child may think that you are too concerned with other things to have time for him. Supervision shows your child that you care.

 **ESSENTIAL**

Good parents never give up supervision, no matter how unpopular and tiring it feels, because to do so would be to give up responsibility and appear to abandon caring.

The Power of Pursuit

With pursuit (or nagging), you wear your child's resistance down by relentless insistence. "I know this is the third time I've asked you to do your chores, and I'll keep asking you until you get them done." Nagging shows parents mean business about getting what they asked. It works. "I finally did the dishes to get my parents off my back. I was tired of being hassled about it."

Pursuit, Not Punishment

Doing homework and doing chores are supervisory issues and should not be subject to punishment for not being done, because they are nonnegotiable. Punishment says, "If you choose not to do your homework, you will be punished." Supervision says, "You have no choice about not doing your homework. You will do it because I will keep after you and after you and after you until you get it done." You don't punish not doing homework. You use supervision to see that homework gets done. As for the haggling and arguing your child does to put off doing what you have asked, that is just an expression of resistance, and the purpose of your nagging is to use your greater power of insistence to wear that resistance down. "You can argue all you like, but I will keep after you and after you until you get your homework done."

The same is true with chores. The child needs to know he or she simply has no power of refusal. Delay will not make these demands go away. Do not give the child a choice over what is nonnegotiable. Punishment says, "If you don't do your chores, a negative consequence will follow. This is your choice. This is up to you." Supervision says, "You will do your chores, and I will keep after you until they are done."

Yelling Cycles

One trap of supervisory pursuit is the frustration parents feel when their request is greeted by endless delay. At last giving in to aggravation from asking repeated times for one simple act of cooperation, they may end up yelling to get what they want, using loudness to show how serious they are and to "force" compliance. If you resort to yelling on a regular basis, you have created a cycle that is a trap.

 **FACT**

> Supervision is too important to get emotional about, because it turns a performance issue (how parents get something done) into an emotional issue (how the child gets parents upset). Supervision works best when it is calm, unwavering, and inescapable.

Both parents and child agree: They all hate the yelling—parents for "having" to do it, the child for having to listen to it. Then why do parents do it? They explain, "Unless we yell, we can't get your attention and cooperation. If you'd just do what we asked the first time, we wouldn't have to yell!" Explains the child, "The reason why I wait until you yell is because by then I know you're getting serious."

Parental yelling models voice raising to get one's way. It empowers the child—he knows he can upset you by delaying. It actually reduces parental influence by causing parents to resort to more emotional intensity than the situation warrants—a simple task or chore needs to be accomplished. In all these ways, yelling is self-defeating.

Be Relentless, but Not Emotional

Supervisory pursuit is most effective when it is unemotional. Therefore, if you find yourself heating up or getting run down in the process of pursuit, take a break for a while, have your partner take up the chase, or simply give yourself time to calm down. Your child needs to know that even though you may be backing off for the moment, you are not giving up for all time.

The issue has not gone away. You will be back. But you will be back on your rational terms, not on yelling terms that undermine your influence and empower the child. Keep on keeping on. Your child will get the message and eventually comply with your request. Children who know their parents won't give up tend to practice relatively immediate compliance. Your relentless insistence will wear down the child's stubborn resistance.

 **QUESTION?**

What kind of supervision works better than nagging?
Prompting. Cheerfully given and helpfully intended, prompting is pursuit with friendly reminders, requiring you to still feel friendly (not frustrated) in the face of protracted delay.

The Power of Surveillance

You also need to check on the child when he or she is away from home. If he thinks he can escape your supervision when he's away from you, you let him know that that is not the case. "I hate it when you chase me down," complains the child. "I can't go anywhere without knowing for sure you won't show up." "That's right," you agree. "I don't much like doing it either, but I expect you to keep our agreements about where you go and when you're coming back. If you don't, then like you say, I'm coming after you. You decide to hang around the playground and not come in when we agreed? Then I'm coming to the playground to bring you home. If that's what it takes for you to know I'm serious, then you can look for me whenever you decide that it's okay to come home later than the time we set."

Surveillance demonstrates to the child that parents are willing to invade the child's world for good behavior's sake. Parents are willing to vote with their actions to show they mean what they say. It doesn't feel too cool to be busted in front of friends by parents who were willing and able to check up on you by tracking you down. Good parents never give up.

Overnights

One common challenge for supervisory surveillance is checking on the child spending the night at a friend's. The early adolescent wants to be able to make his or her own social engagements and resents parents checking with host parents to see if these arrangements are as okay as they have been told. "You don't have to call his parents and check. I told you it's okay with them if I spend the night. Are you trying to embarrass me?" No, you are trying to make sure adequate adult supervision is in place.

After all, you know about the temptations of forbidden freedom in early and midadolescence. There can be a lot of temptation for your child to lie about where she's going and then sneak out with her friends to do something that you would not have given permission for. By checking on overnight arrangements, you can prevent two kinds of end runs. A "single end run" is when your child goes over to a friend's house overnight and they both sneak out from there. A "double end run" is when two children tell respective parents they are each going to spend the night at the other child's house, and then both children do neither and take off for a night of forbidden adventure.

If your child insists on sneaking out after hours from your own home or running off, you need to create hot pursuit. If you think you know where the child might be hanging out, go after the child. If you think a child's friend might know, call that friend and ask to be told (promise not to tell your child how you found out). If you have no idea where the child might be, call the police and report a runaway. In many cases police will be able to find and return the child to you. All these acts of surveillance let the wandering child know that freedom not responsibly earned will be freedom denied.

Electronic Surveillance

Many parents take advantage of the technology of cell phones, pagers, and instant messaging devices, using them to keep watch on their child. In fact, some children will complain, "You only gave me the cell phone to keep up with where I am!" "That's right," reply the parents. "We expect you to keep the cell phone with you at all times partly so you can call us if you have need, and partly so we can check in with you if we have need. Answering our calls whenever we call is one condition for allowing the freedom we give." Parents use electronic pagers to the same effect.

 **ALERT!**

If your child's life seems to take an inexplicable downward turn into trouble, you might want to start checking where your child goes on the Internet, checking e-mail, site visitation, instant messaging, and chat room activity to see to whom and about what your child is communicating. If you lack the technological expertise to do this yourself, get a more computer-knowledgeable friend to help you, or even pay someone who has these digital tracking skills.

Privacy Issues

What about your child's privacy? Privacy is a privilege, not a right. If your child is keeping you honestly and accurately informed, and is conducting life in a responsible manner, you allow privacy because you are being given grounds for trust. But if he is lying to you, breaking agreements, violating rules, and he's not explaining this behavior to you, then the child has forfeited any right to privacy. Now your invasive surveillance into the child's "private" world is justified. How can you help if you don't know what is going on?

So maybe you discover chat room data that outline plans for sneaking friends over when you are still at work and your child is supposedly safe at home, alone, after school. "You spied on my chat room?" Your child is outraged. So parents explain, "You cannot electronically communicate without leaving electronic tracks that we can trace if we feel you are not telling us all we need to know about what is going on." Never give your child more online (Internet) freedom than you are prepared to supervise.

Home Alone

How can you be at home when you are not? This may sound like a riddle, but it isn't. When outside commitments, particularly jobs, pull parents away, a child is often left at home alone. School's out for the day, or for the summer, but you still have to be at your job during the day. Unless you can afford additional child care, you have to find ways to supervise your child when you are gone from home.

The time between the end of the school day and when parents arrive home can give a child left alone plenty of opportunities to get into trouble. It's not that this freedom is so pleasurable that the child gets into trouble. In most cases, trouble occurs because the opposite is true. This weekday freedom can be painful. It can be even more painful during long vacations.

Too Much Time Alone?

How can freedom be painful? The answer is boredom. The problem with too much time alone is boredom—the child has more freedom than she knows how to fill. Having "nothing to do" creates a serious state of discomfort for many children. This discomfort is a kind of loneliness stemming from not being able to entertain or accompany oneself in a satisfying way. "I don't know what to do with myself!"

ESSENTIAL

If you don't set some terms of safety and responsibility for keeping your child directed when you are away and he or she is home alone, your child will set his or her own terms, which may not be to your liking. "Home alone" is freedom that requires supervision.

Boredom is painful for a child because boredom feels lonely. The child is at a loss for how to connect with himself in a satisfying way. "I hate being bored!" "I hate having nothing to do!" These are true statements about true pain. It is to escape the pain of boredom that many children turn to trouble. Boredom is a staging area for trouble where children play follow-the-leader with impulse to find something to fill the void of emptiness they feel.

Increasing Parental Presence

The danger of protracted boredom is stated strongly here to give parents warning. Don't leave your children at home alone with nothing to do. Create a supervisory parental presence for your child when you can't be there with him. After school before you get home, on the weekend, over vacation—whenever your child is left at home alone—give him some things to do that not only keep him busy, but that also remind him that he is still accountable to you for his behavior. Give him:

- A schedule to follow.
- Activities to engage his interest.

- Tasks that you approve and he enjoys.
- Some household chores to accomplish.
- Personal work requirements, like homework, to get done.
- Specific times to communicate with you.
- Specific times to expect communication from you.

For safety's sake, telling the child what to do is as important as telling the child what not to do (no friends over without a parent there, no cooking, for example). Posting the requirements, rules, and schedule for time home alone is a good idea. The poster represents the parental presence. Obviously, when your child uses this alone time well, you want to praise this show of responsibility.

The Messy Room

When your child hits early adolescence (around the ages of nine to thirteen), the freedom to keep a "messy room" often becomes an issue between parents and child. The disorderly room often feels like an affront to parents (and even more so to stepparents) who want a more orderly space in which to live. Their corrective response then becomes an affront to the adolescent who sees a power issue worth fighting for. Who should decide how the young person should live in his or her own personal space?

The Power Struggle

What started as a simple matter of spatial disorder becomes a symbolic struggle over who's in control. "It's my room!" declares the adolescent. "I should be free to live in it any way I want!" "Wrong," counter the parents. "It's our home, and you will live according to the standards of household order that we set!" So the battle lines are drawn for a conflict of mess up versus clean up that can unfold over many years.

For the adolescent, there can be a lot at stake in asserting the right to the messy room—issues about independence, individuality, and opposition to parental rules. As a statement of independence, the child seems to say, "I can live in my own space on my own terms!" As a statement of individuality, the child seems to say, "I am going to be different to live with than when I was a child!" As a statement of opposition, the child seems to say, "You have no right to dictate your standards of order in my personal space!"

 **FACT**

Accept it: The messy room is emblematic of the adolescent age, a strident statement that your son or daughter feels entitled to live on his or her own, more independent, terms. "It's my space, it's my decision, it's my life!" Your supervision tells him or her that this freedom is not yet to be.

So, do you want to let the messy room go? Do you want to just accept it as a byproduct of this more assertive and rebellious age? Or do you want to make a supervisory response instead?

Supervising the Enforcement of Your Rules

By insisting on regular room cleanup, you let it be known that your child must live on your terms so long as he or she is dependent on your care. You are letting your child know that a "trashed" room causes you to feel your home is being trashed, and you won't have that because you work to keep a home and keep it up. If your child knows you will keep after the small responsibilities like cleaning up a messy room, he or she will also know that you will keep after big stuff like obedience to major rules.

Now your child has a suggestion. "Just close the door and keep out and the mess won't bother you." Don't accept that offer. If you allow the child's mess to keep you and your supervision out, your child may start keeping things in the room, and conducting activities in the room, that you do not want in your home or in the child's life. At the age of awakening curiosity about the grown-up world, such freedom can be abused—as license to explore and experiment with the forbidden.

If your child asserts, "This is my room and you can't come in without my permission," your answer needs to be "Yes" and "No." Yes, you should knock before entering if the door is closed. Yes, you should allow the room to reflect the changing identity of your growing child (decoration within your tolerance for acceptable expression). And yes, you should value this decoration as a window into understanding your child's changing interests and identifications as he or she continues to grow.

 **ESSENTIAL**

Remember that if you have a child with a high degree of ADD/ADHD characteristics, having a simplified and orderly personal space to live in can help that child gain better control over the conduct of his or her life, because a messy room only adds chaos to a life that is already hard to keep organized.

This said, you also have to state conditions under which you will say no to the right of privacy. As you do with freedom for electronic communication, so do with freedom of personal space. Privacy remains a privilege, not a right. Use privacy to conceal or to conduct the forbidden, and that privilege is lost because personal freedom is being abused. If your child is inexplicably changing for the worse at home and is getting into significant trouble at school or out in the world, but she refuses to discuss with you what is happening, asserting your right of "search and seizure" in her room may uncover private communications or paraphernalia that disclose what is really going on.

Resisting Schoolwork

As children enter adolescence between the ages of nine and thirteen, they start to assert more independence and test the limits of your authority. In the process of this change, it is very common for a child who previously was very motivated academically to slack off doing his schoolwork in favor of spending more time focusing on the social aspects of his life—connecting with friends and being popular. Energy that used to be invested in doing homework is now diverted to talking long hours on the telephone and to instant messaging over the Internet. In consequence, less interest in accomplishing schoolwork can lead to lower grades.

In most cases, this performance drop doesn't really mean the adolescent no longer values doing well academically, it just means he or she doesn't want to do the work to do well—class work, homework, reports, projects, papers, and studying for tests. So it is at this juncture that parents often find themselves confronted by a number of antiachievement behaviors. The most common ones are:

- Not delivering deficiency notes sent home to parents, or intercepting them in the mail.
- "Forgetting" or lying about homework assignments.
- Not turning completed homework in.
- Not finishing class work.
- Being disruptive by socially talking out and acting out in class.

Knowing What *Not* to Do

All these misbehaviors are very easily remedied by parents who are willing to take a stand for the adolescent's best interests against what he or she wants. Two things to avoid, however, are becoming emotionally upset or resorting to rewards or punishments to encourage different choices. Although both techniques can work with a young child who wants to please and who will work for material incentives, they tend to be counterproductive with the adolescent, who often courts parental disapproval to accredit independence and may resent your efforts to control those things that he or she wants.

Grades are too important to get emotionally upset about. Growth is just a gathering of power, from dependence to independence, the job of parents being to help their adolescent gather that power in appropriate ways. It is not appropriate for parents to give the adolescent power to get them upset over grades, because then the academic focus is lost and the young person wins influence over parental feelings. "I can really push my parents' buttons by doing poorly in school."

ALERT!

> Getting upset over grades turns a performance issue into an emotional encounter, showing the adolescent that he can control your emotions by his willingness to work or not work at school.

Grades are too important to reward or punish over. Parents often mistakenly believe that offering an adolescent some significant payoff for good grades will be seen as a reward. But by this age, the time when earning systems can work is over. In fact, most adolescents will see it as a threat that they resent. "If you say you're going to give me five dollars for an A, that just means that if I don't get an A, I don't get the five dollars."

Likewise, taking away some resource or freedom until grades improve usually just makes the child resist more than cooperate. "I don't care what you take away, you can't make me do my work!" When parents reward or punish grades, they turn a performance issue into a power struggle with their adolescent.

Supervision to the Rescue

What then are parents supposed to do? Just stand by and watch their early adolescent fail from failing to do the work? Sometimes that's the advice middle school teachers give to parents. "Don't be overprotective. Let your child fail and learn responsibility from the consequences." But unless the adolescent has the maturity to correct himself, buckling down to bring his grades up, he will only learn to adjust to failure, treating failure as okay when it is not.

After all, a report card is meant to act like a mirror, the adolescent seeing in that written evaluation an adequate reflection of his or her capacities. Parents' saying to an unmotivated adolescent who is capable of A's and B's, "All we want you to do is pass," is tantamount to giving up on their child, withdrawing faith in his or her high potential, and abandoning their responsibility to influence school behavior. But if emotional upset and rewards and punishments tend to be ineffective with the early adolescent achievement drop, then what are parents to do?

The answer is supervision—pursuit and surveillance. Remember that the early adolescent, unlike the child, does not want parents showing up in his or her world at school. Desire for social independence means keeping parents out of his or her society of peers. Now the company of parents at school feels like a public embarrassment because he or she should be able to handle school without their interference. To which parents reply, "We have no desire to interfere at school so long as you are taking care of business. However, if you do not do schoolwork and if you are acting inappropriately in class, we will extend our supervision into your school to help you make better choices."

So, if deficiency notices are not delivered home, you may want to say something like this: "Since information for us that the school entrusted to you was not delivered, we will meet with the teacher together, and you will have the opportunity to explain why the notice failed to reach us and what you are going to do differently next time so it does."

If your child has told you he had no homework, when he really did, you may want to say something like this: "Since you said you had no homework, but you did, we will meet with the teacher together. At that time, you will have the opportunity to explain why you said there was no homework when there was, and what you will do differently the next time so we will be told the truth. And this weekend, before you get to do anything you want to do, you will have to complete the missed assignments, turning them in for zero credit because they are now late." And if homework still is not reliably brought home, you promise to meet your child at the end of the last class and together make the rounds of the teachers to pick up all homework.

If the adolescent does the homework but chooses not to turn it in, you may want to say something like this: "Since you can't manage to turn your work in, we will go up to school with you and together walk the halls and make the rounds of all your teachers to make sure your homework gets turned in."

 **FACT**

Doing homework has more to teach than practice in a given subject. By faithfully doing their homework, children are learning to develop a work ethic—the ability to make themselves do work they do not want to do, a discipline that will serve them well in later life.

If the adolescent is talking out or acting out disruptively in class, not completing teacher assignments, you may want to say something like this: "Although this is not something we want to do, we are willing to take time off from work and sit together with you in class to help you behave appropriately as the teacher asks."

Usually, an early adolescent will not welcome any of these options, considering them outrageously invasive, preferring to correct self-defeating conduct instead. What you are saying in each case, however, is that so long as self-correction does not occur, you are committed to steadfast supervision because you know improved school performance will ultimately cause the adolescent to feel better about him- or herself, as well as keeping choices open in the future.

Supervision shows your child that you care enough to keep after her with pursuit and surveillance so she takes care of responsibilities that are in her best interests to accomplish. Supervision (nagging and checking) is honorable work and needs to be faithfully done.

CHAPTER 12

Punishment: The Third Factor

PUNISHMENT CAN BE PERSUASIVE. Applying a negative consequence can discourage repetition of wrong-doing. "I had to work to earn the money to pay for replacing the window I broke, so I'm going to stop throwing the ball around inside the house."

It's best to avoid physical punishment like spanking because it mostly demonstrates that when you are bigger than another person, it's okay to hit them to get out your anger or to get your way. Spanking teaches hitting.

Instead, there are three other kinds of negative consequences you can enforce—isolation, deprivation, and reparation. The goal of each of these is to cause the child to think about why the consequence has been imposed and to consider not committing that significant misbehavior again.

However, if punishment is the only corrective parents use, not only does it place undue negative influence on the relationship, but also it erodes the power of punishment itself. "My parents will just ground me some more, so I don't care. It's no big deal."

Good Parents Never Back Off

Constructive punishment is confined to applying some negative consequence that the child does not want. It is a symbolic response that you should reserve for

violations of significant family rules and agreements. Punishment is meant to make a strong corrective statement. It is designed to catch the child's attention, cause the child to rethink what happened, and to discourage the child from committing that forbidden action again. "Because I stole some money from my mom's purse, I not only have to pay her back, but I also have to keep her purse in my room at night, count out to her how much money it contains before I go to bed, and repeat the count the next morning to make sure no money's missing before giving it back to her. And I have to do this for two weeks! She doesn't want me to forget what I did wrong. She wants me to learn to be trustworthy around her money." The purpose of punishment is to use a negative consequence to teach the child what not to do again.

 **ESSENTIAL**

> The purpose of punishment is never to do physical or emotional injury. The purpose is simply, when a major infraction of the rules occurs, to apply a consequence that has enough symbolic value that it convinces the child not to repeat this offense again.

Good punishment is an art. Like the example given above, it can be creative, where parents design a consequence that gets exactly to the point of demonstrating what they don't want to happen again, and by implication what they do. In this case, they want trustworthy behavior regarding the parent's money.

Testing Rules

To some degree, the relationship between parent and child is between rule maker and rule breaker. In adolescence this can become a kind of serious game, the teenager testing rules, getting around rules, and disobeying rules to gain more freedom while parents, in the interests of their child's safety and responsibility, monitor compliance and respond to violations that occur.

Children grow up partly within and partly outside their parents' rules. No child is 100 percent obedient or tells parents the whole truth all the time. For parents, significant compliance and adequate communication are the best compromise they are going to get.

Sometimes in ignorance, sometimes on impulse, sometimes under the influence of friends, sometimes under the influence of substances, sometimes with deliberate intent, your child will break one of your rules. When violations occur, parents back up their rule with a negative consequence. Never back off a significant rule by simply letting a violation slide—that weakens the rule that you made for your child's good. Just as you reward compliance with appreciation and more freedom, you penalize serious infractions with punishment. Sometimes a good talking-to is sufficient (putting a stop to unauthorized "borrowing" of your possessions); other times more is required (making restitution for damaged property).

The Emotional Side

Even when a major rule has been violated, you may be tempted to not apply punishment for a couple of reasons. First, your child will feel unhappy receiving the consequence, and you may want to avoid causing that unhappiness because you can't stand making your child "feel sad." And second, feeling unhappy about a punishment he or she doesn't like or doesn't agree with, the child may decide to punish you back with disapproval or anger. "I'm never going to like or talk to you again. Ever!" To avoid this punishment from your child, you may prefer to let the violation go. In the first case, you don't want to cause your child pain; in the second, you don't want to receive pain yourself.

To prevent their child from getting angry at them for the punishment they have given, parents will sometimes declare, "You have no right to get angry at us for being punished when you brought the punishment on yourself by doing wrong!" They want to shift responsibility for punishment to the child. But that is wrong. The offense was the child's responsibility. The decision to punish and the choice of consequence selected were the parents' responsibility. Children often feel angry when punished by their parents, making punishment an unhappy experience for both child and parents. However, major rules that are violated with impunity are not rules at all. At most, they are guidelines parents don't really mean. Good parents never back off.

ALERT!

> Parents who regularly punish or threaten punishment to get routine consent, punish too much. To be effective, punishment must be selective. The more often punishment is used, the less corrective power it has. "Big deal, you're going to ground me from the TV again."

The Power of Enforcement

Enforcement means that parents give children major rules to live by, monitor compliance, and back up those rules with punishment should violations occur. By punishing violations, parents communicate that the rule is real and that they meant what they said when they set it.

Particularly when the child is young and small and helpless, it is hard for parents to be careful in the exercise of their authority and not abuse the greater size and strength that they possess. To some degree, most parents will occasionally abuse their adult power by allowing fatigue, frustration, or impatience to result in a raised voice, threatening words, or an angry touch. How can these responses be abusive to your child? Because they can scare the child, and fear of parents violates the child's sense of safety with the people on whom he or she most depends for love and care.

The Problem of Fear

Punishment is a strong exercise of corrective power. It demonstrates how significantly a parent can affect conditions in a child's life. The purpose of punishment is to teach a lesson, not to make a child afraid. This is why punishment must be decided rationally, not emotionally. You must give punishment with careful thought, not with impulsive anger.

If you choose to enforce rules by using punishment to instill fear, you may get strict obedience, but it will be at excessive cost. Your child will learn to:

- Distrust you because you are not safe.
- Keep interpersonal distance from you in order to be safe.
- Manipulate you with dishonesty in order to keep safe.
- Love you less as he or she comes to fear you more.
- Have contempt for you as a bully, not respect for you as a leader.

Using intimidation to influence obedience can be at the expense of closeness now and friendship later as adult children may remain distant or estranged, resenting the parent who once ruled their life by exploiting their fear.

QUESTION?

Should a child be "made" to say she's sorry about wrongdoing as a condition for fulfilling the punishment even though she has no remorse?
No. Forcing an apology is like begging for a compliment. Both are worthless unless sincerely given.

The Problem of Anger

Unless you express your anger separately from the punishment you give ("I'm going to tell you how angry I am now, and later we'll discuss the consequence for what you did"), you are likely to overreact and overpunish. Allowing emotion to do your thinking for you, you will declare a punishment that is either too extreme or is unenforceable, having to later retract or modify it, which shows that you didn't really mean what you said in the first place: "You're grounded for the next year!" In addition, your anger may obscure the lesson you want learned, and the child may think he or she is being punished because you are angry and not because of the bad choices he or she made.

Remember, anger can seem like the enemy of loving feelings. In the moment, anger over what is "wrong" can obscure appreciation of all that is "right." For young children, parental anger is threatening for this reason. Because an angry parent seems not to be a loving parent, it takes some learning for the child to understand that such anger is only a passing interruption, and that parental love is here to stay.

What Anger Teaches Children

To be punished by an angry parent causes the child to associate his parent's anger with being treated in a powerfully aversive way. "Stop playing and go sit in the corner!" yells the parent, furious after tripping over a toy that shouldn't have been left at the bottom of the stairs. "And don't you dare get up until I tell you!" When punishment is linked with anger, fear of the parent's anger can be what the child learns.

And if you blame your child for causing you to get angry, then you have just encouraged guilt in your child over your chosen emotional response (for which only you are responsible). Now the child mistakenly believes, "It is my fault my parents yelled at me!"

Particularly with children under six, you must remember how much physically larger and more powerful you are than they, and how important being safely attached to you is for their emotional security. Larger size amplifies the power of parental anger.

Very young children can be frightened by parental anger or their own: Where did loving feelings go and will they return? It takes repeated safe experiences to trust that anger does not destroy love, it only temporarily interrupts the flow of loving feelings. This is why anger over a disciplinary violation needs to be expressed safely by talking it out and not acting it out. Far better for parents to explain anger by verbally describing their feelings in response to what occurred than by acting those angry feelings out in criticism, threats, yelling, or temper. Anger is the enemy of effective punishment because it can cause parents to overpunish, and it can frighten the child with fear of loss of love. Remember: Most rewards for good behavior are given for the child's sake, but most angry punishment is given for the parents' sake.

ALERT!

Punishment is no time for anger. Punishment is a time for due deliberation to select an appropriate consequence that will deter some wrongdoing from happening again. Waiting to find out what the consequence will be is part of the punishment.

When it comes to managing anger at your child for misbehavior, keep your hands to yourself.

- Never lay angry hands on your child to get his or her attention.
- Never use angry hands to "shake some sense" into your child or to express your frustration.
- Never use angry hands to threaten physical harm.
- Never use angry hands to strike a child in retaliation for wrongdoing.

For the parent of an adolescent, anger can sometimes be sticky. After unsuccessfully trying to settle a disagreement with an obstinate teenager, anger can stick around because the angry parent is holding on to it, refusing to let go. "Even though it's over, every time I think about the argument with my son, I still feel angry! He just wouldn't see things my way! And he wouldn't let me have the last word!" Carry unresolved anger forward from one infraction to the next, and you risk overreacting in the next disciplinary encounter.

Are You an Anger-Prone Parent?

Anger is functional. It is a healthy response to perceived violations of your well-being. It empowers you to make an expressive, corrective, or protective response. "When you use sarcastic name-calling to put me down, I feel hurt and angry. As your parent, I don't do that with you, and I don't want you doing it with me."

But what if you or your family feels that you are angry too much of the time? You may be anger prone if you have one or more of the following characteristics.

- The more controlling you are, the angrier you will get when you do not get your way right away. A child's delay will be treated as an act of defiance.
- The more judgmental you are, the angrier you will get at those who do "wrong" in your eyes, or who refuse to accept that you are "right." A child's disagreement will be treated as an act of disrespect.
- The more sensitive to hurt you are, the angrier you will get at unintended offenses from others. A child's forgetfulness will be treated as a personal affront.

Anger-prone parents tend to train a child to become anger prone like themselves, or to become someone who grows up frightened of anger, avoiding or placating other people's anger to his or her personal cost.

 **FACT**

If you hold on to anger too long, it will turn into resentment, doing you much more harm than it does the child at whom you're still angry. Alcoholics Anonymous has a saying worth remembering: "Resentment is like taking poison and waiting for the other person to die." Anger can be toxic to the holder.

If you are prone to one or more of these characteristics, either at home or behind the wheel of a car with a child as passenger, work on changing them. They are not fixed. You can change them with practice. Try to be less controlling by letting go more control. Tell yourself, "I don't have to have everything go my way to be okay." Try to be less judgmental by evaluating conduct of other people less. Tell yourself, "I don't have to be right about everything." Try to be less sensitive to insults by not taking so much that happens in your life so personally. Tell yourself, "I don't have to take offense at what I don't like if I don't want to." Discipline is most effective when it is free from anger.

The Limits of Punishment

Punishment should be used only to enforce major violations of rules, not to correct continuing irritations (such as not picking up clothes, leaving the refrigerator door open, playing music too loud) or minor infractions (such as not doing chores, continuing to talk on the phone after hours, not doing homework). These more minor instances of misbehavior should not be dealt with by punishment since they are guidance and supervisory issues. Lying, sneaking out, hitting another person, stealing, driving under the influence of substances, skipping school—these are the kinds of choices that constitute major violations that may require punishment as a corrective.

Defeating the Purpose

Although not a part of instruction, as a correction, punishment is still meant to reform misbehavior: "Don't do that again." It should never be used, however, as an excuse to do a child harm. It should not be used to inflict physical or emotional injury. Use punishment for giving hurt, and its corrective power becomes corrupted. The good intended is ignored for the bad received. "What I learned is that when I do wrong, my dad thinks he has the right to beat up on me!"

Parents who use sarcasm to embarrass, who use humiliation to shame, who use criticism to devalue, who use temper to intimidate, who use suffering to arouse guilt, or who use anger to inflict bodily harm are not only destructive, but they are self-defeating as well. Any corrective benefit is far outweighed by the cost of compliance. Abusive parents care about only the obedience they are getting and the frustration or anger they are expressing. They do not care about the injury they are doing or the love they are losing. For punishment to be corrective, it needs to be rationally thought out, not emotionally driven.

Parents are most at risk of losing control of themselves when they feel they are powerless to affect their child. In reality, no parent is 100 percent without influence, because no child is 100 percent uncooperative. Parents always have some platform of positive influence to build on because the child is always doing some things they want and is not always doing some things they don't want.

 **ALERT!**

> When it comes to punishment, knowing what *not* to do is as important as knowing what to do. Don't punish to get back at your child, to get even with your child, to make your child feel bad, to show your child who's boss, to relieve your frustration, or to satisfy your anger.

Physical Punishment

Although many parents would deny it, physical punishment is given more often for the parent's sake (to relieve frustration or take out anger) than it is given for the child's sake (to discourage repetition of misbehavior). In general, physical punishment such as poking, pinching, squeezing, spanking, swatting, popping, slapping, and belting proves only four things to the child: "You are bigger. You are stronger. You are entitled to be violent. And when I'm a grownup, I will be entitled to act the same way."

The means (the physical hurt), not the end (learning not to repeat the offense), becomes the major message. "All I learned is that because he is bigger and stronger, my dad can slap me around!"

Add up all the arguments for spanking, and together they do not outweigh this one objection against it. Spanking teaches the child that hitting is okay if you are bigger and stronger and cannot get what you want any other way. Spanking teaches hitting.

External and Natural Consequences

Because your child spends time outside the family system, there are external rules that he or she must follow as well. There are social laws and school regulations, for example, and when they are violated, official authorities may apply punitive consequences such as arresting a teenager for public misbehavior or requiring a child to serve detention for skipping school. These are external consequences applied by outside authorities in punishment for violating social or school rules.

There are also natural consequences that arise when a child's choice leads to an unintended outcome that punishes the original decision that was made. A thoughtless or careless decision can lead to a punitive outcome. Thus, a wallet carelessly left out in the locker room at school is missing after athletic practice. No driving the car now until the driver's license is replaced. The adolescent has been taught a lesson on taking care of personal belongings.

As a general rule, don't double punish misbehavior when your child has already suffered external consequences enforced by other authorities or has experienced adverse natural consequences. Instead, sympathetically help your child learn from what occurred.

Of course, there are exceptions to the general rule of not double punishing when external or natural negative consequences have already occurred. For example, if your adolescent gets charged with a DWI (driving while intoxicated), you certainly want the boy or girl to experience whatever legal, educational, and community service consequences apply. In addition, however, you may also want to take away or restrict driving privileges until your child can demonstrate that he or she can be more responsible about using the car. In this case, the external consequence is not punishment enough.

At home, there are three kinds of punishment parents can use that have different kinds of corrective power: isolation, deprivation, and reparation.

Isolation as Punishment

Isolation is temporary exclusion. The most common form of isolation is taking a timeout. The purpose of isolation is not to ostracize or reject the child. It separates the child from a problem situation and begins a process to help the child commit to correcting misbehavior so he or she can behave acceptably in the family once again. The corrective sequence is separation time, thinking time, and discussion time. Then it is time for re-entry.

 **FACT**

Children learn from experience only when they accept the consequences of their decisions. They won't learn from consequences so long as they deny responsibility for personal choice or parents deal with those consequences for them.

Effective Timeouts

After getting the child out of the problem situation, a timeout should last only however long as is needed for the child to be willing to calm down, think out, and then talk out what happened and what he or she will do differently from now on. So, after your daughter has grabbed the remote control from her younger brother (whose turn it was to select a TV program) and hit him when he objected, you give her a timeout to think about what she did. She violated the family rules against taking and hitting. When she feels she has calmed down, has thought about the incident enough, and feels ready, the girl lets the parent know she is ready for discussion. This means she feels ready and willing to talk about what happened, why it happened, and what she's going to do differently the next time so this misbehavior doesn't happen again. This discussion must be to the parent's satisfaction. This is where correction gets to have instructional value.

Fully discussing what happened helps to further develop talking-out skills, which may then (you hope) be used to work out solutions in the future instead of just acting out objections. Of course, once the timeout sequence has been completed, you should make sure a positive focus on the child and your relationship has been restored.

Keeping Emotions Down

Timeouts also serve another purpose. When either you or your child, or both of you, are getting too emotionally intense about an issue in a disagreement, declare a mutual timeout to cool each of you down. The purpose of this timeout is to reduce emotional arousal, restore perspective, and then reopen the discussion, both of you now prepared to "start over" in a more reasonable manner. During this cooling-off period, you have each had a chance to think up some new ways of approaching the issue at difference between you.

One very positive timeout for all concerned can be a family vacation—a time when normal tensions, differences, and hostilities are often suspended because the usual duress of living together does not apply. "We fight all the time at home, but we had a great vacation!" You've taken everyone out of normal family context, where now the focus is simply on having fun. A vacation can be a "getaway." For a lot of families, it is a timeout that pays enormous dividends, reminding all concerned how they really value and can enjoy each other's company.

Deprivation as Punishment

Deprivation is passive punishment. Deprivation is a strategy for taking away a usual access or social freedom the child values as a consequence of the child's having done a major wrong. Access usually has to do with the privilege of using such things as the computer, the telephone, the TV, the car. Freedom has to do with the permission to socialize on normal terms with friends or engage in normal outside activities.

ALERT!

Sometimes in their severity, parents will strip the child of everything he or she values doing to show how serious (or angry) they are. Extreme deprivation is a big mistake. Now the child has nothing left to lose, so the parents have inadvertently set their son or daughter free.

The longer you take either privilege or permission away, the more you lessen the power of deprivation, because the child just adjusts to doing without, but not without building resentment. For this reason, deprivation needs to be short term to be effective. "For breaking curfew last weekend and not even calling in to explain why you wanted to be late, you have to stay home next Saturday night. You need to keep your agreements with us, and check with us when you want those agreements changed." Never use deprivation to take away any outside activity that serves as a pillar of the child's self-esteem, such as church youth group activities or sports. That kind of deprivation is self-defeating. Impose some other social restriction instead.

Deprivation of access can create a lot of anger because the child may see it as a betrayal. What he or she assumed were basic rights—using the telephone and computer, for example—turn out to be privileges given so long as good behavior is given in return. Extreme use of access deprivation can create significant distrust. "You're only letting me drive a car so you can have that to take away. Well, I don't want to drive a car! I'm not playing the take-away game with you anymore!"

Grounding In

Deprivation of freedom, or "grounding," is usually used with adolescents who are at the age of growing up when social freedom matters most of all. Grounding can include prohibition against going out with friends, against having friends over, against talking on the phone, against computer messaging with friends, or against engaging in normal social or recreational activities. Long-term grounding tends to be counterproductive because you turn punishment into a prison sentence, your home into a prison, your child into a prisoner, and yourself into a prison guard as grounded as the prisoner you keep. Over a sustained time, you will both learn only to resent each other.

Long-term grounding in also can have a social cost you do not want your child to pay. If you take your child out of social action in his or her peer group long enough, the child will lose standing in that social order. On returning, he or she must struggle to reclaim a place that may have been taken by someone else, your child now more subject to peer pressure than was the case before. So if you ground your child by keeping her in this weekend, don't ground her from the phone unless you want her kept out of the loop of information that keeps everyone else connected.

Grounding Out

In extreme cases, there is another kind of grounding, different from "grounding in." Suppose your late adolescent refuses to stay grounded in the house for violating curfew and decides he can leave home anytime he likes and stay gone as long as he wants. At this time, you may elect to use "grounding out."

So you say something like this to your unruly teenager: "You need to know that we are operating a home, not a prison. As you have made perfectly clear, you can leave whenever you choose and stay out as late as you like. We can't stop you. However, although leaving is up to you, permission to return is up to us. When you want to return, you can call us. From the time of that phone call, you must stay away from home twelve hours for the first curfew infraction, twenty-four hours for the next curfew infraction, and so on. During that time you will have to make your own living arrangements, and you cannot come by and pick up clothes or any other belongings. At the end of this grounding out, we will meet you at an outside location at a time of our convenience to discuss the rules you must be willing to live by if you want to return to live at home."

Reparation as Punishment

Reparation is active punishment. "Because you did something you weren't supposed to do, you will have to work off the infraction before you get to do anything else you want to do." There are a number of advantages to using reparation as a punishment.

- The child has to actively do something to work off the infraction.
- While working off the infraction, the child has time to think about the violation that led to this consequence.
- When the infraction is worked off, the child goes forward with a clean record, confident that the particular infraction has been paid for and will not be brought up by parents against him again.
- Parents assert much more authority with reparation than by deprivation because they are getting the child to do some work they are glad to get done.

Sometimes parents will keep a list of usual household jobs (not regular chores) that need to be done posted on the refrigerator that can be referred to when they need to apply a punishment. "You need to get this job done to our satisfaction before you are allowed to pursue anything else you want to do that requires our assistance, support, or permission." One reason parents tend to prefer deprivation to reparation is that reparation takes supervision, and deprivation does not. However, of the two, reparation is the more effective punishment.

The Negative Attention Trap

It's not just that positive parental attention has more power to shape positive behavior in a child than negative parental attention does, but excessive negative attention can help make some misbehavior immeasurably worse.

Misbehaving for Attention

Consider the following situation. Despite her father's nightly warnings about not spilling at supper, the child manages to spill something at least once a week, causing the father to regularly lose his temper in response. "What's the matter with you? How many times do I have to tell you to be careful! What do I have to do to get you to watch what you're doing? You keep on spilling when you know how angry that makes me!"

Then, after the child has been sent from the table, the father wonders, "Why does she keep spilling when she knows how upset I get?" Of course, the father's answer is in his question. That's why the child spills: to get a lot of negative attention from her father.

Why would a child want negative attention?

- Negative attention feels better than no attention.
- By his reacting so predictably when she spills, the child gains apparent control over his behavior.
- There is a sense of power in being stubbornly uncorrectable.
- When he acts so extremely upset, she knows she has his full attention.

Changing Negative Focus into Positive Focus

Actually, if her father had kept a clearer focus, he could have discovered what to do from what he sometimes did. The key to his understanding is that, in anger, he believed she spilled "every night," but on emotionally sober reflection, he realized that some nights, like last night, she doesn't spill. Why not? What contact did he and she have before supper? For whatever reason, last night he had the energy to play a game before they sat down to eat. Maybe, because she was given positive attention to begin with, she didn't need to provoke bad attention in the end.

If the father wants to escape this negative attention trap, he needs to change a number of his behaviors.

- He needs to withhold negative attention when the spill occurs and not act upset or get angry.
- He should shift into neutral emotionally, and matter-of-factly ask the child to clean up the spill, asking her to get a kitchen sponge and mop it up, thanking her when the cleanup is accomplished.
- He should give some specific instruction about how to hold the glass differently to avoid spilling.
- He should find dinner table behaviors in his child to which he can give positive attention, like praise for helping set the table.
- He needs to increase other kinds of positive attention he generally gives the child away from the dinner table, like taking special time to play with her when he gets home from work.
- He needs to use his own affirming responses to encourage desirable behavior in his daughter, replacing a punitive relationship with a positive one.

ALERT!

Critical parents, who find it easier to get angry than to give approval, are easily caught in negative attention traps.

Although the child is used to getting angry attention from her dad, she will quickly prefer getting loving attention from him instead. When it comes to parental attention, negative may feel better than no attention, but positive feels better than negative.

CHAPTER 13

Exchange Points: The Fourth Factor

O F THE FOUR BASIC DISCIPLINE techniques, using exchange points has the most training value. Its immediate value is causing the child to understand that there is a connection between getting what he or she wants and giving parents what they want. Its further value is preparing the child to understand how to conduct healthy relationships in the future.

Children depend on a parent for a great deal of support that they take for granted. They believe that providing resources, permission, help, and a variety of services is what a parent is "supposed" to do. With this assumption in mind, children can come to feel entitled to live in a one-way relationship where they do most of the getting and the parent does most of the giving. As far as children are concerned, that's okay.

For the parent, however, "all give and no get" can feel tiresome at best and exploitative at worst. So, when children next make a request or expect to be provided some service, the parent makes sure there is an exchange that takes place. "I am certainly willing to drive you over to your friend's home, but before we go, I want ten minutes of your help folding the laundry." This is an exchange point: when you do something for your child and your child does something for you in return. It tells the child now and teaches the child for later that giving in relationships goes two ways, not just one.

Good Parents Get as Well as Give

When parents work an exchange point to withhold what the child wants until they get what they want, they are not being punitive, because they are neither being negative nor threatening to take anything away. Using exchange points is positive: "I will be glad to do what you want after you have done for me."

Protests your child, "I promise I'll bring in the trash like you asked when we get back. Can't we go now?" No. Unless the child has proven extremely faithful about keeping agreements, you may want to treat promises as false currency. It is performance that counts. "First the trash; then the ride."

Anytime your child asks or expects something of you, that is a potential exchange point. Think before you act, and ask yourself, "Was there something I requested from my child that has not yet been given?" If so, don't give until you get. "I'm glad you're here on time for supper, but before you sit down to eat please pick up your backpack from the hall and put it in your room like I asked."

 **FACT**

> Without some give-and-take by both parties, an unhappy disparity can trouble any caring relationship. When one party does most of the giving while the other party does most of the taking, the giver is likely to start building resentment toward the taker.

Consider chores, those regular household tasks that your adolescent regularly puts off doing as long as possible. You've tried guidance, explaining why you need chores done in a timely way, and words have proven ineffective. You've tried supervision, nagging and nagging to get chores done, and that has proved exhausting. You don't believe delaying chores is a major rule violation, so you are not going to waste the big gun of punishment on a small but persistent aggravation.

Instead, you just wait until the next exchange point. Because of all the ways your teenager is dependent on you, it will come around soon enough. And when it does, you let your child know how happy you will be to do what is wanted, but not until the chore you wanted done has been accomplished first. Good parents get as well as give.

The Power of Mutuality

Beyond getting what you want at the moment, using exchange points with your child teaches your son or daughter to practice mutuality in the relationships that matter to them. Mutuality involves making three basic exchanges.

- **Reciprocity:** This means both receiving and giving contributions to each other's well-being. So, your child has been trained not only to receive help from you, but to give help to you as well.
- **Compromise:** Both parties must be willing to sacrifice some self-interest for each other and for the greater good of their relationship. Your child has been trained to cooperate by giving up some wants to get along with you, just like you do with your child.
- **Consideration:** Both parties must make an effort to be respectful of each other's sensitivities. So, your child has been trained to not knowingly go after your emotional sore points, those issues about which you are easily hurt, just as you avoid sore points with your child.

With this training in mutuality in place, not only is your child appreciated at home, but also he is usually well received out in the world, where his interpersonal skills will help him create and sustain two-way relationships with other people as well.

Someone You Can Enjoy Living With

Children who have practiced and acquired the three exchanges of mutuality are generally nice for parents to live with, and nice for others to interact with out in the world. But what about children who have not been so trained? What about those children who have been trained to believe in one-way relationships? What about children who have been trained by insecure, compliant, indulgent, or neglectful parenting to believe all the benefits in a relationship should go their way? What about children who have modeled themselves after a parent who mostly gets and takes at home, but rarely gives? In those cases, you get a child who is no pleasure for parents to live with.

One of the risks of adolescence, when children typically become extremely preoccupied with their own needs and become more intent on satisfying personal wants, is that parents may allow training in mutuality to lapse. And when they do, they get a teenager committed to one-way behavior: "My needs come first," "Things should be done my way," and "My feelings matter more than anyone else's." Unless you want to live with a teenager who believes these statements and acts on these beliefs, you better insist that the three exchanges of mutuality be met all the way through the teenage years.

 **ESSENTIAL**

One goal for parents is to raise a nice child—one who, for the most part, they enjoy being around because he or she has been trained by their discipline to live in a two-way relationship with them.

A spoiled child is a child who has not been taught to practice mutuality in relationships. Spoiled at home, he or she is usually spoiled for meaningful relationships away from home, because who wants to put up with such a self-centered human being? Using the exchange points to teach a child mutuality serves the parent's needs now and the child's needs later on.

Predictable Behaviors in Parents

Sometimes you may become stuck in a negative exchange with your child. There's giving and getting, all right, but you're not happy with the exchange. Lately, whenever you refuse to let your teenager do what he wants, he gets angry, gets in your face, raises his voice, and loudly demands that you change your mind. The question is, why does he act this way? The answer may be the same as the answer to this question: "What does he predict you will do in response?"

If you want to change this exchange, you may choose to react in a different way than what he expects. To do this, first identify what your specific behaviors are when you react to his aggressive challenge to your refusal of his request. Suppose, on reflection, you can name three: you stop talking, you feel your facial expression become tense with fright, and you back away. Maybe you even back off your decision. These behaviors are part of what he predicts will happen—he knows that by getting in your face he can intimidate you. He is getting the response he wants in this exchange.

Now you decide to change your reaction. Next time you refuse a request and he gets in your face angrily and loudly, you choose to act very differently. You smile, you put your hands on his shoulders, you pull him toward you, you kiss him on the cheek, and you start telling him how much you love him when he acts this way. Instead of showing him intimidation, you are giving him affection. And you let your decision stand.

Wow! This is not the response he was predicting or working for. If this is how you're going to act when he gets in your face, maybe he won't get in your face again, because this is not the response he wanted.

Taking Back the Initiative

Sometimes the exchange between parent and child becomes one-sided in terms of who initiates most interactions in the relationship. For example, parents describe the relationship with their prickly adolescent like this: "We're always waiting to see what she's going to do next. When she comes home from school, is she going to act pleasant or unpleasant, be in a good mood or bad mood, like us or criticize us, do what we ask or refuse? We get so nervous around her, not knowing what to expect. We're the parents, but she's really in charge."

 **FACT**

> Mutuality means that both you and your child share the responsibility of taking initiative in the relationship. If your child's focus and agenda rule the relationship, you can end up feeling resentful of your child. Make sure there is a two-way exchange.

And the parents are correct. Their daughter has come to control the initiative in their exchange. They allow her actions to keep them constantly on the reactive. Essentially, she dictates the agenda and focus in the relationship. The question these parents continually ask themselves is, "What does she want from us now?" The question they need to start asking themselves is, "What do we want from her now?"

When this kind of imbalance in the exchange with their child takes place, parents can take back the initiative by claiming a more active role in the relationship, making more requests of their own, putting the teenager more on the reactive. So, as soon as your daughter storms in the door from school, instead of waiting to see what she's going to do, greet her with several pieces of family business you need from her. Your actions immediately put her on the reactive for a change. After arguing (which you most likely predicted), she flees to her bedroom in protest, but there is no getting away. For the next week, whenever you see her, give her something you want her to do, give her feedback on something, or ask her questions about her life. Now more balance in initiative has been re-established.

Being Part of the Family

A family is a system of interpersonal relationships in which the welfare of the whole depends on contributions by the members. If no one contributed, the family would cease to function, each member simply going his or her own way. Although parents are the major contributors, children must be taught to make significant contributions as well.

If mutuality functions well in your family system, then everyone understands that relationships are supposed to work two ways and not just one. If exchanges ("I do for you, you do for me") are taken for granted as a natural part of family life, then your child is more likely to accept the principle that to get, he or she has to give. The lesson of mutuality you want to teach your child is that it takes a personal investment to get something from his parents (except, of course, your love and acceptance).

 **ESSENTIAL**

Household membership requirements like daily cooperation, chores, and helping out teach the child that to get benefits from parents there is a simple rule: no investment, no return.

Parents who demand no household membership requirements only increase a child's belief that relationships are supposed to be one-way. Then they get angry with the "selfish" or "inconsiderate" or "unhelpful" child, but that anger is misplaced. They are better off getting angry with themselves for not training their child to be a stakeholder in the family system by becoming a contributing member. Ultimately, it is the child who suffers, because noncontributing children will become noncontributing adults, who often have difficulty sustaining healthy relationships.

CHAPTER 14

The Only Child

I N THE UNITED STATES TODAY, more than 20 percent of parents have an only child. There are many reasons why families with only children are more common today than they were fifty years ago, when larger families were the norm. People are marrying later (or divorcing earlier), are waiting longer to start families, have more and better access to birth control, and often make career choices that don't accommodate having more than one child. Many parents are also simply deciding that one child is family enough.

From the outside looking in, only-child families seem easy to run. After all, parents don't have to divide affection, attention, and resources between children. They don't have to put the needs of one over the wants of another. They can give undiluted and undistracted focus to the well-being of a single child. They don't have to put up with the normal bickering and push and shove that are part of how siblings tend to get along. And they don't have to mediate conflict between rival children to determine who started it, who did what to whom, who is right, what is fair, who gets to do what, who gets the most, or who goes first. All in all, parenting an only child seems like a relatively simple proposition—except it's not.

Special Concerns

Parenting an only child is high-pressure parenting. Having an only child means their son or daughter is first

and last child in one, so parents have only one chance to do parenting "right" (providing for all their child's needs) and not do it "wrong" (causing their child hurt or harm).

As mothers and fathers try to parent "right," they can develop high performance standards for themselves, and to avoid parenting "wrong," they can become prone to worry. The outcome of high standards and high worry is conscientious, labor-intensive parenting—carefully weighing responsibility to make sure their only child is served well and not badly by their decisions. Add to performance and worry pressures the parents' desire to please the child, to make him or her happy, and parents of an only child have a complicated job on their hands.

ALERT!

Sometimes, what parents of an only child see as "discipline problems" turn out to be "excess pressure" problems in disguise. Be careful not to increase the pressures that already exist for your only child to please you and perform well.

The problem with this high-pressure parenting is that parents cannot demand a lot from themselves without communicating that concern for high performance and, more important, that example of high performance to their child. Fundamentally, what parents give their only child is who and how they are. Thus, seeing parents striving to do their best, the only child usually follows suit, striving to do his or her best, too.

Living in a family where everyone tends to be so dedicated to trying hard, not doing wrong, and pleasing each other, the only child can be extremely sensitive to instructional discipline (being given more responsibility to live up to) and correctional discipline (being faulted for failing to follow family rules or meet family expectations). Parents of an only child need to be particularly sensitive about how they give discipline, doing it in such a way that they do not increase special family pressures under which their son or daughter already labors.

To provide low-pressure discipline, parents of an only child need to understand what these special family pressures often are. Instructional discipline creates pressure on your child to master more of what parents want learned, when the child is usually already striving to learn all he or she can. Corrective discipline communicates parental displeasure to a child who usually wants more than anything to please his or her parents.

Parental Peer Pressure

From the beginning, an only child (who has only his parents for social company at home) is subject to peer pressure from parents that, in most cases, they aren't even aware they are exerting. The law of peer pressure is the same everywhere: conform to belong. Espousing the ruling norms of a group allows an individual member of that group to fit in, get along, and become a member in good standing. So the only child adjusts to parental ways, accepts parental terms, imitates parental actions, and acquires parental beliefs in order to be in good favor. In response, parental acceptance and approval is given.

A common example of similarity to parents is the only child's becoming schooled in "grown-up" behaviors at an early age, developing precocious verbal and social skills that can set him apart from other children his age.

 **FACT**

An only child often prefers the company of younger children (to be able to be in social control) or the company of adults (to be able to use "grown-up" social skills). The rough and tumble—sharing and compromise—of playing with her own age group may feel less comfortable to them.

"It's like having a third adult in the house," parents proudly declare when describing how their eight-year-old can comfortably socialize with their friends. And that statement of pride feels rewarding to the child, affirming that he has done well by acting so much like them.

To avoid intensifying parental peer pressure when you discipline, you can avoid certain behaviors that can make inevitable discipline harder to bear.

- Don't push for similarity to parents too strongly or praise it too highly.
- Don't make similarity to parents a condition for receiving approval.
- Don't treat infractions with disapproval, just with disagreement.
- Don't blame the child's misbehavior on being "different" from parents.
- Don't use isolation or exclusion from parents as a punishment.

Emotional Enmeshment

It's obvious to say, but important to remember, that parents and an only child grow extremely close emotionally. Their bonding is rooted in spending so much time together, keeping each other exclusive social company at home, caring so much for each other, and coming to know each other so intimately. Typically, their relationship is emotionally sensitized—parent and child being able to tell, without words, how the other is feeling. It is difficult to mask true feelings from each other.

Feeling Tied to Each Other

Difficulty with such closeness arises when some degree of emotional enmeshment occurs, when parents and child tie their own feelings to the well-being of each other. Having thoughts like the ones below is often a sign of emotional enmeshment.

- "I feel okay if you feel okay."
- "If you don't feel okay, then I don't feel okay."
- "If you don't feel okay, then I need to help you feel okay."
- "If I am unable to help you feel okay, then I won't feel okay."

ESSENTIAL

Emotional enmeshment comes at the expense of emotional independence that allows one person to feel bad without the other automatically feeling bad in response, obliged to "fix" the unhappy other so both can feel okay.

How Discipline Reinforces Attachment

Since some degree of emotional enmeshment is very common between parents and an only child, both instructional and corrective discipline can increase the pressure on this intense attachment. Instructional discipline can cause the child to believe that learning to act how parents value (school achievement, for example) will cause parents to feel good about the child and themselves. So when parents look at A's on a report card and declare, "We must be doing something right!" the child links her personal performance to her parents' well-being. "How I do determines how my parents feel." Better for parents to have simply said, "Congratulations for how well you've done!" and express satisfaction for the child, rather than with themselves.

Correctional discipline can be hard for both you and your child to deal with, making you both unhappy with yourselves and for each other. A parent may say, "It hurts me to give correction because I know it hurts my child." The child may say, "It hurts being corrected because that means I have failed to please my parents and now they are unhappy because of me." When disciplining your only child, try to get adequate emotional separation in the relationship by objectively dealing with the offense: "This is what happened that we don't want to have happen again."

Keeping the Pressure Off

To keep possible emotional enmeshment from unduly pressuring the delivery of discipline, there are some guidelines you can follow.

Don't praise your child by attaching your good feelings about yourself to his or her good behavior. Statements such as "We're proud of you" or "You make us feel so proud" may increase pressure on the child to believe, "How well or badly I do determines how well or badly my parents feel about themselves." Better simply to say, "Good for you!"

Don't blame your child for "making" you unhappy, angry, disappointed, or otherwise upset by his or her misbehavior. Your child is responsible only for her actions. Your emotional response is your responsibility, not your child's.

Never use sensitive knowledge confided by the child against him when you discipline. If you do, you will betray the heightened intimacy and trust that usually exists between an only child and his parents.

Don't deny unhappy feelings or tensions connected with discipline of your only child who is too sensitive not to sense something is "wrong" and will only imagine the worst.

End all corrective discipline, after the child experiences the consequence, with reconciliation of feelings and reaffirmation of your love.

The Tyranny of Pleasing

Parents and their only child usually have a mutual admiration society. Each side gives the other such high approval ratings that neither one can stand the thought of displeasing the other, or of not pleasing the other enough. This makes giving discipline especially hard to do and receiving discipline especially hard to take.

Excessive pressure to please each other can create a "tyranny of pleasing," where both parent and child are too focused on getting approval from each other, and neither wants to do anything to cause disapproval. In order to please parents, the child may choose not to express an honest opinion or pursue an authentic interest they have spoken against. In order to please their child, and not cause unhappiness, parents may be unwilling to make unpopular demands and set healthy limits.

To reduce this tyranny of pleasing, parents should clarify for themselves and their only child the difference between love and approval. Love is a given. It is rooted in the parents' unconditional acceptance of the person their child is. Approval is earned. It is rooted in the parents' responsibility to conditionally evaluate their child's performance and to communicate how well or badly he or she is making decisions in life.

 **ESSENTIAL**

Explain to your child that love and approval are not the same. Love is a constant; approval varies with evaluation of the child's behavior. Love does not guarantee approval any more than disapproval means a loss of love.

Just because you have a responsibility to evaluate your child's development does not mean that you must express disapproval when the child misbehaves. In fact, what you need to do is neutralize your evaluation when giving correction by expressing it not as disapproval but as disagreement, as follows: "We disagree with the choice you have made, here is why, and this is what we need to have happen in consequence."

To keep the tyranny of pleasing from making it harder to discipline, you can communicate that your relationship will, for both you and your only child, of necessity, be displeasing sometimes, and that's okay.

- "We don't always have to agree with what each other believes."
- "We don't always have to like each other to get along."
- "We can disapprove of each other's actions and still love each other as much as ever."

- "We will both sometimes make decisions to please ourselves that we know will be displeasing to each other."

The Expectation for Return

Parenting an only child is high-investment parenting. All that you have to give as parents is devoted to the welfare of a single child; all your hopes and dreams for parenthood ride on the shoulders of how that child grows through life. On the one hand, what you give, you give freely out of love. On the other hand, being human, you do have some expectation of return for all the caring, time, energy, resources, and effort you have put in. The high investment parents make in an only child often comes with a high expectation of return.

Sometimes, often in adolescence, the only child will object to the pressure he feels to make good on that return. "When you say you only want the best for me, what you really mean is that you want the best *from* me. The more you do for me, the more I'm expected to do for you, and most of all that means doing well! It's like I'm supposed to live my life to make you look good!"

Instructional discipline (with its focus on learning to do what's right) tells the child that there is even more return that she is expected to give. Corrective discipline (with its focus on wrongdoing) charges the child with failing to provide the return of good behavior that parents expect.

Communicate to your only child that he or she does not owe you an unblemished and stellar performance in return for the dedicated care and support you provide. "All we expect from you is what we expect from ourselves—an honest effort to do what's right that results in a mixed performance of good decisions and bad, because none of us is perfect, only human."

In addition, do not declare disappointment when your only child doesn't do as well as you want or does what you have forbidden. That just painfully intensifies the sense of obligation that he already feels with additional guilt.

Also, do not use the words "should" or "ought" when administering discipline. Both words just encourage feelings of duty in a child who already carries a strong sense of obligation to you.

 **FACT**

The only child's tendency to imitate and please parents who are very sensitive and understanding makes for a harmonious childhood most of the time. Come the more stormy adolescent years, however, more correction is often called for, and that can be unexpected and painful for parents to provide.

Unrealistic Standards of Performance

Being peers with parents not only leads the only child to develop more grown-up speaking and social skills at an early age, but it also causes the boy or girl to feel more adult from the adult association. In consequence, the child will frequently lay claim to adult-like standing in the family. Not intimidated by parental authority (and often not by adult authority in general), the only child often feels he or she is entitled to significant, if not equal, participation in family decisions.

Unhappily, this is where a self-imposed performance pressure can begin for many an only child. By presuming comparable standing to parents ("If I can act their equal, then I should have equal say"), the only child carries this equation one dangerous step further: "If I can act equally grown up, then I should be able to perform equally well."

But the child is not an adult, and so these standards are inappropriate and unreachable. "I can't do it as well as you," moans the only child when the more experienced parent does something better. Then, to ease this frustration, the parent may respond, "Don't be so hard on yourself, you're just a child." But this is not what the only child wants to hear, and now she feels put down and assigned inferior standing in the family.

To help keep your only child's unrealistically high standards from making your discipline even harder to take, soften the stands you take by making honest explanations. "When we want you to take on additional responsibility, that doesn't mean you are not trying or working hard enough. It just means that as you grow there is more self-discipline to learn." "When we call you down for not doing what we feel you should, or for doing what we feel you shouldn't, that doesn't mean you don't do anything right. In fact, it's the exception that proves the rule: most of the time you conduct your life extremely well."

ALERT!

Signs that your only child is putting unreasonable demands on himself include: an intolerance of anything less than outstanding personal performance, extreme frustration with mistakes, severe self-criticism, and despondency after losing in competition or failing to achieve a goal.

Falling Away in Adolescence

Most parents of an only child are not well prepared for their child's transformation into a more private, self-centered, critical, resistant, conflict-prone, limit-testing person at adolescence, who begins to prefer the company of friends to that of parents. Inexplicably and unpredictably cut off, parents can feel rejected, abandoned, lonely, angry, scared, or out of control. Come their only child's adolescence, parents who already feel disconnected and out of favor often have to assert more corrective discipline than they have ever had to assert before, and the child does not appreciate this attention.

Changes in Adolescence

In adolescence, the only child—who was encouraged from an early age to be assertive and self-directed, to act adult, to be independent, and to speak his or her mind—becomes more powerfully resistant than parents often expected and can immediately handle. Consequently, they may feel overwhelmed by this period of their child's life. Now they have to strengthen the stands they take as parents and face the displeasure of their child for doing so. In the process of assuming this hard responsibility, they can experience a tremendous sense of loss. Parents sorely miss the old closeness, mutual enjoyment, and uninterrupted harmony between them and their only child. "What's wrong?" they wonder. Nothing. Their beloved child has just become a difficult adolescent.

 **ESSENTIAL**

> Parents who themselves were compliant growing up, and who have been used to having a compliant only child, may have to toughen up considerably when their considerate and cooperative son or daughter becomes a more self-centered and strong-willed adolescent.

Although most only children tend to be conservative when it comes to dangerous risk taking, they still have a lot of growing to do in adolescence. To some degree, this part of their development requires them to push against and pull away from parents, to separate from childhood, to experiment with becoming different, and to begin claiming more social independence from family.

Common Fears

This "falling away of the only child" in adolescence can be very painful and scary for both the parents and the child. For the parents, it usually comes as a surprise. Since their child had previously followed a path they understood, approved of, and supported, they rarely, if ever, had a reason to correct or restrain the child. But now the child may let high grades fall from lack of effort, may object more to helping around the house, may let new friends lead him astray, and parental attempts to communicate with him may often yield outbursts of anger or sullen silence.

For the child, claiming this rebellious independence is expensive. There are a number of common fears that trouble the only child in adolescence.

- If she pushes her parents too hard in conflict, she might be pushing away their love.
- If she pulls too far away socially from parents, there may be no getting back to the old closeness they once had.
- By expressing individuality that was not there in childhood, she may be risking rejection or at least disapproval by her parents.
- Rebelling against her own interests for independence may harm the future he or she had been working for.

On the reassuring side, remember that when your only child falls away in adolescence, he or she usually does not fall very far into dangerous experimentation or social disobedience. Most only children fall away just far enough to let their "bad" side out to claim necessary independence from childhood, but not so far that they fall into serious trouble.

Usually, your momentary losses of the old childhood relationship are less traumatic than the losses that your child fears—loss of loving standing in parental eyes, and loss of standing in his or her own.

Your Role as Parent

So what are you to do? Gently and firmly, you have to keep providing instructional and corrective discipline so your adolescent always has a clear and open choice to return to a productive path after some episode of falling away has taken place. This must be done noncritically and with love.

Once again, nonevaluative correction is essential. "We disagree with the choice you made not to finish your project. But that was your choice. However, we still expect that you will get it done, now having to do it this weekend and hand it in late for a lower grade. As always, we believe you have everything it takes to perform the way you want in school. Our discipline in this matter is only intended to show you our support."

What can you say to your only child when he is poised on the threshold of adolescence? Perhaps, something like this: "We are about to enter a time when we will grow more apart, when there are going to be more disagreements between us, and that's very common in adolescence. As parents, we are sometimes going to take stands for your best interests against what you want, and you will not agree with our decision. As our child, you are sometimes going to do what you believe is called for in a world of friends you best understand, and we will not agree with your decision. We just need to handle these disagreements in safe and constructive ways, and still enjoy enough times together for us to stay mindful of the love we have for each other."

CHAPTER 15

Discipline Changes with Age

A S YOUR CHILD GROWS OLDER, your approaches to discipline must change in response. Your son or daughter develops greater capacity for language, for understanding, for judgment, for responsibility, for spending more time away from home, and for getting into normal trouble. Different techniques will work best with different ages. This chapter gives you an approximate schedule for changing your approaches to disci-pline as your child grows from infancy through adolescence. All the specific approaches mentioned have either been described more fully in previous chapters or will be discussed in those that follow.

Early Childhood (Up to Age 3)

At the outset of childhood, a little child needs to feel securely attached to you, safely trusting in your love. She must be shown how to behave, because she hasn't mastered language enough to learn through verbal explanation. Fortunately, it is easy to show a very young child how to behave, because, like the young of many mammals, he or she naturally imitates parental actions.

Giving Instruction

By example you instruct. Through your endlessly repetitive modeling, playing, and gaming, your child gradually acquires early disciplinary skills and understanding, like how to pick up and how to eat, that you want learned. Your child wants to learn to act like you.

FACT

No single discipline technique works all the time for every parent with every child in every problem situation. Parents need many approaches to discipline from which to choose and must keep choosing until they find one that is effective for that particular child at that particular time.

Patience and positive attention are the order of the day. Rewarding desirable behaviors with expressions of pleasure and praise encourages the child to repeat those behaviors, because pleasing parents is what children at this age most want to do. Thus, rewarding a desired behavior like toilet training when it happens works far better than trying to force that behavior on a child with insistence, frustration, anger, or expressions of displeasure when it is not done. "I'm going to make him sit there until he does it!"

When you're trying to teach a disciplinary skill and your child goes off task, throwing a spoonful of food instead of placing it in her mouth, redirect her attention to some other interest. Then bring it back to eating instruction and let re-education begin again. Children are not one-trial learners. Maintaining a sense of play and having patience with practice is necessary for instruction to succeed. Reward both effort and success with positive attention. The formula for disciplinary teaching at this age is:

PLAY + PATIENCE + PRACTICE +
POSITIVE ATTENTION = PRODUCTIVE INSTRUCTION

Giving Correction

Because parental displeasure, particularly anger, can be so frightening at this early age, parents need to rely as much as possible on instruction to instill discipline, keeping correction as a last resort. If, however, redirecting and re-educating is not working with your child's throwing objects or hitting, you can gently but firmly correct with a headshake "No."

Stooping down so your eyes are level with your child's, with a serious but not angry expression on your face, clasp the child's hands in your own, and look the child in the eye. Then, in a firm, clear voice repeat the word "No" several times, shaking your head each time you do. Wait a few seconds to see that the child has registered your message by looking at you seriously, then give the child a hug, smile, and resume your normal positive interaction. If further correction is required to stop the offending behavior, just keep repeating the headshake "No." Do not resort to more severe correction.

Late Childhood (Ages 4–8)

Once your child has acquired the power to understand speech and to speak, you can provide an enormous amount of instructional discipline through verbal description and explanation. There are all kinds of how-to skills to master that teach a host of responsible behaviors—from dressing, to basic hygiene, to memorizing home address and phone number, to doing household chores, to following directions of many kinds.

In addition, during this time, you begin teaching two important foundations for later discipline—cooperation and responsibility. You teach the building blocks of cooperation by training the child in listening and attending, giving to get, keeping agreements, and being of service to the family. You teach the basis of responsibility by helping your child learn the relationship between choice and consequence, connecting a decision he makes with the outcome that follows. For example, when she makes choices that you approve of, she gets a positive response from you. Likewise, if she makes a choice you do not approve of, she learns that she will receive a correction from you. "You can influence my reactions with your actions," is the lesson you now start to teach.

You also get to work on helping your child learn to become a two-step thinker. Step one is the child's acting on what he or she wants based on impulse. Step two is delaying impulse long enough to apply judgment, to determine if it is really wise to act to satisfy that want. The two-step sequence you want your child to learn is to question his or her motivation: "Am I willing to wait long enough to think about what I want to do to make sure it is wise?"

 **ALERT!**

A timeout can be a useful intervention. It removes the errant child from the problem situation, gives him time to think about his choice and the resulting consequence, and obliges him to talk out what he should do differently the next time before the timeout is over.

At this age, earning and counting systems can be powerful disciplinary tools with children. Earning systems give the child a way to earn specific rewards based on specific positive accomplishments. "Since you did all your chores on time this week, you have earned taking a friend out to eat this weekend." Counting systems put the child on notice with a warning that if her unwanted behavior continues for the full count of three, for example, then she will suffer a specific unwelcome consequence. The child is given a chance to change her behavior before you enforce the consequence.

Transition into Adolescence (Ages 9–10)

Around age nine, your child starts to enter adolescence, when he'll want more personal and social freedom. You must specify under what conditions you will be willing to risk giving more independence than you currently allow. You do this by creating a freedom contract, which spells out the terms your child must meet before you'll consider granting more freedoms.

The freedom contract is explained more thoroughly in Chapter 16. In short, there are six conditions to the freedom contract, all of which must be currently satisfied before more freedom is considered.

- **Believability:** Your adolescent is giving you adequate and accurate information about what is going on in his or her life.
- **Predictability:** Your adolescent is keeping all agreements, promises, and commitments with you.
- **Responsibility:** Your adolescent is taking good care of business at home, at school, and out in the world.
- **Mutuality:** Your adolescent is living on two-way terms with you, doing services for you just as you do services for him or her.
- **Availability:** Your adolescent is willing to openly discuss any parental concerns you have at any time.
- **Civility:** Your adolescent communicates with you on respectful terms, even when you disagree.

Early and Midadolescence (Ages 9–15)

For most parents, more frequent and more serious discipline problems begin during the first two stages of adolescence. For example, your son or daughter may start "forgetting" unwanted obligations, become more argumentative, test limits and rules, ignore schoolwork, delay compliance with chores, experiment with the forbidden, sneak out after hours, and lie, to name a few of the unwelcome changes that commonly occur at this more oppositional age. In response, you need to use a variety of disciplinary responses to convince your adolescent to do what you want, and to discourage your adolescent from continuing to do what you don't want.

There are four common strategies that can influence the kind of behavior you would like to see. First, use guidance as a persuasive technique. Through giving continual feedback to your adolescent about what is working well and not so well in his or her life, you provide a constant, caring reference for constructive conduct. If he misbehaves significantly, he should know that, regardless of what other consequences he suffers, he will always receive a good talking-to that will last as long as it takes for you to state everything you want to say on the subject. Your continual feedback operates as a compass to guide responsible decision-making.

 **FACT**

> When you give instructional discipline, keep it specific by focusing on the behaviors you want or do not want to have happen. When you give corrective discipline, keep it non-evaluative: "I disagree with the choice you have made, here is why, and this is what needs to happen in consequence."

Second, close supervision is effective discipline. Through nagging and checking you will make sure that your adolescent is taking care of her responsibilities at home and at school, and you will use your relentless power of insistence to wear down your teenager's resistance to carrying out tasks you have asked to be done.

Third, provide structure by setting rules—but only ones that you care enough about to back up with punishment if they're violated. Punishment is not for undone chores or homework. Those are supervisory matters. Punishment is for major rule violations, meant to catch the teenager's attention, cause the teenager to think about the violation, and discourage the teenager from repeating it again. Having to do something to work off the infraction (reparation) tends to be a more powerful corrective than simply losing a privilege or freedom (deprivation).

And last, use exchange points to acknowledge the teenager's dependence on parents for a host of resources, permissions, and services that the parent may withhold until the noncooperative teenager relents and does what the parent has asked. The parent is basically saying, "I am happy to do for you what you want, but before I do, I want you to do something for me."

These four disciplinary interventions have larger social lessons to teach. Throughout adult life there will be authorities telling the child what to do and what not to do, keeping after the child to see these demands are met, expecting cooperative contributions from the child, and punishing infractions if social rules are violated. Family experience approximates what it will be like living in the larger social system for your child.

Late Adolescence (Ages 15–18)

When the time for leaving home and living "on one's own" approaches, usually coinciding with graduation from high school, your teenager needs to be adequately equipped for managing more social freedom and responsibility than he or she has ever known before. The goal for parents during the late adolescent years (ages fifteen to eighteen) is to prepare their teenager for this challenging transition by dedicating much of their instructional discipline during high school to imparting all the knowledge and skills he or she will need to successfully step off into independence, making this next step as small as possible.

ALERT!

Growth is a gathering of power from dependence to independence, and a parent's job is to help the child gather that power in appropriate—not inappropriate—ways. In the late adolescent period, you are helping your child develop life skills that are appropriate for assuming more independence.

How is this preparation to be done? Use the late adolescent years to help your teenager acquire the varied responsibilities that support self-sufficiency. You have a lot of disciplinary work to do, and you can do it in three ways.

Begin by considering what responsibilities your teenager will need to master to function more independently in the world after leaving your care. Thus, when your teenager enters late adolescence, at about the age of fifteen, ask yourself a question: "What exit responsibilities need to be in place when our teenager leaves home to successfully master more independence?"

Then you list all the essential knowledge and skills you can think of that support independence. For starters, there is hunting and interviewing for employment, creating and living on a budget, basic car maintenance, filling out an income tax form, using public transportation to get around town, and managing a debit or checking account. This is the curriculum you want to teach during late adolescence to get your teenager responsibly equipped to successfully manage the demands of greater independence that are ahead. Having made your list, decide at what point, and through what means, during the late adolescent passage you are going to teach these skills. You have a lot of instructional discipline to provide during the high school years.

Next, ask yourself another question: "What services and resources do we provide for our teenager that he or she can learn to provide for him- or herself?" Explaining to your teenager what you are going to do and why, one by one you begin to transfer these responsibilities to your child, giving instruction as needed. In this fashion, your teenager now undertakes responsibilities for shopping, doing personal laundry, making personal medical and dental appointments, earning money, and paying for more personal expenses, for example.

 **ESSENTIAL**

By the end of high school, you want your teenager to be able to say, "I am used to taking care of most of my own needs."

Finally, you focus on your teenager's senior year and try to approximate the full social freedom he or she is soon to have after leaving home. Turn over all responsibility for schoolwork, for managing any earned and allowance money, for nightly curfew, for example. You do this because, while your teenager is still living with you, you want to see how he or she manages the degree of freedom of self-determination soon to be available. If your teenager can't handle all parts of it, you want to be there to help him or her accept responsibility for how ill-advised choice leads to unhappy consequence. During senior year, you want to put your teenager's degree of responsibility to the test. Of course, while still living with you, the young person still has to keep you adequately informed and meet various household membership requirements, like chores. Your job is not to punish bad choices, but help your teenager learn from mistakes.

Trial Independence (Ages 18–23)

Living away from home and out in the world for the first time, with a host of more grown-up responsibilities and commitments that must be met, the final stage of adolescence is the most challenging of all. Most young people do not find an independent footing right away. They break commitments, they struggle with responsibilities, they lack direction, and they usually make some choices that get them into trouble. Now your disciplinary help is needed more than ever, but it needs to be only instructional, not correctional. Your son or daughter is too old to accept or benefit from your punishment, but is not too old to profit from what you have to teach. This openness to your instruction, however, depends on your altering your traditional role as managing parent. You have to give up that role for another: mentoring parent. As a mentor, you are no longer in the business of trying to "make" your young person mind your discipline. You are not even in the business of telling him or her how to behave.

Instead, you are someone to whom your young person, after choosing his or her way into trouble, can come for advice about ways to choose his or her way out. You are now safe to come to because you do not express disappointment, worry, criticism, anger, or despair. You are a source of ideas, of wisdom from life experience. And you are a source of empathetic and encouraging support, expressing complete confidence that your son or daughter has what it takes to cope with the unfortunate situation a poor choice has created, to find a way to responsibly resolve the situation, and to learn from mistakes. Mentoring is your disciplinary role during the final period of your child's growing up.

QUESTION?

What do approaches to discipline in early childhood and trial independence have in common?
At both extreme stages of growth, parents are best served relying on instructional discipline, rarely, if ever, resorting to correction.

Once a Parent, Always a Parent

Even when your child is all grown up, you retain a position of influence in the young adult's life—not as corrector or instructor but as an example. You continue to serve as a model for how to cope with the challenges of life. When adversity strikes, when value conflicts test your integrity, when you speak up or stand up for personal beliefs, when your way of life shows positive value, this power of example has meaning for your adult child.

Most important, throughout their adult lives, you can, if you want to, be an appreciative audience, understanding support, and cheering section for all your grown children as they journey through their own challenges in life. Remember: What they wanted from you when very young, they continue to want from you when they grow older, too—affirming, attentive, approving responses to some very basic human needs.

"Watch what I can do!"

"Listen to what I did!"

"Tell me what you think!"

You see, that's all that your child ever really wanted from you in the first place: to shine in your eyes.

CHAPTER 16

Disciplining the Teenager

ADOLESCENCE IS that ten- to twelve-year process of growth that begins when your child separates from childhood around age nine to thirteen and finally graduates into early adulthood in his or her early to mid-twenties. It is a long process of transformation that manages to turn a dependent child (at the outset of adolescence) into an independent young adult by the end.

The Hard "Half" of Parenting

Adolescence is a process fraught with ups and downs, progress and backsliding, harmony and conflict, obedience and disobedience, truth and lying, certainty and surprise. In adolescence, to some degree, your child will try to push against your authority (opposition), pull away from your company (separation), and get around your rules (manipulation). All of these behaviors are your child's way of asserting more individuality, establishing more social independence, and creating more worldly freedom to grow. Breaking old boundaries to achieve this individuality, independence, and freedom usually involves breaking some of your rules and agreements in the process, and so more discipline problems are created.

Adolescence is not a punishable offense. It is a process of growth. Therefore, do not punish teenagers for the process (communicating with you less, for example), but do hold them accountable for how they manage this process (keeping you adequately informed, for example).

Parenting the Teenager

As your child goes through the stages of adolescence, your job as a parent is to create enough structure, restraint, and responsible demand to help provide a safe and healthy passage through a complicated and risky period of growth. No matter how hard your son's or daughter's childhood may have been for you, the hardest part of growing up—adolescence—comes last. Although you may spend less time with your teenage son or daughter than you did when he or she was younger, you spend much more time thinking about your child as he or she begins to venture out into the larger, and more dangerous, world outside of family.

 **FACT**

> Adolescence wears the magic out of parenting. As a parent you will likely become more and more disenchanted with the abrasive teenager, and your teenager with you. This is how it should be—conflict over freedom wears down the dependence between you until by the end of adolescence you are each willing to let the other go.

Although it can be confusing to both child and parents, adolescence is an orderly process. Certain changes, tensions, conflicts, and problems tend to unfold in a predictable fashion. For example, a more negative attitude and more limit-testing come early in adolescence, followed by intense preoccupation with self and urgency for freedom by midadolescence. The desire to act all grown up and the anxiety about true independence is typical of late adolescence. And the last phase of adolescence—trial independence—tends to be plagued by a sense of relative incompetence and a lack of direction.

None of this means that you are destined to experience agony when your child enters adolescence. About one-third of children seem to go through adolescence without a ripple, smoothly navigating the separation from childhood, the experimentation with becoming different, and the departure into independence all within the tolerance limits of their parents. These are the "easy" teenagers. Another third tests some limits and breaks a few rules, but it's nothing that firm and understanding parents can't correct. These are the "typical" teenagers. Finally, however, there are a final third who push extremely hard against parents, who must take hard stands in response. There can be significant family conflict as a result, and sometimes counseling for the family can be helpful. These are the "challenging" teenagers. Most families don't get more than one "easy" teenager, so don't expect the same smooth passage for all. If your first child grows slowly through the teenage years, you are likely to have another who is more adventurous and in more of a hurry.

The Problem of Hurry-Up Growth

As you know, some adolescents physically mature more swiftly than others do. Puberty comes early and growth changes unfold fast. Suddenly, they look several years older than other kids their age. The thirteen-year-old boy looks like a young man, or the thirteen-year-old girl looks like a young woman. They are physically out of step with their peers, which often attracts the social attention of older adolescents who assume that the early-maturing adolescent has the interest and capacity and experience to go with his or her more grown-up looks. Adults jump to the same conclusion: "He looked old enough to handle the responsibility; how was I to know he was so young?"

A young person who matures early faces unrealistic expectations from the outside world that he or she feels compelled to meet. The message these young people get from peers and other adults is, "Act as old as you look because that is how we will treat you." So, older boys start showing social interest in your daughter, who is really just in early adolescence but who now feels pressure to grow up fast.

Or consider another hurry factor—social advancement. Suppose that when your athletically gifted fourteen-year-old enters high school, she is encouraged to work out with varsity players. As a freshman, she is suddenly put on the same peer level with seniors. Treated as one of them, your midadolescent is routinely exposed to the company of older adolescents and is even invited to their social occasions. Academic acceleration can have the same effect.

Early maturity and social advancement can create pressure to grow up faster. It is unrealistic to expect and demand that a thirteen-year-old who looks seventeen, and who is being treated as a seventeen-year-old by the world, be content to tolerate the limits and restraints of someone four years younger. It is unrealistic to expect and demand that a ninth grader who hangs out with seniors is going to be content acting like a freshman. In either of these cases, you are probably going to do some letting go earlier than you anticipated.

However, your willingness to let go requires that your teenager confide in you more than he or she anticipated. That is key to your disciplinary stand. To get this early freedom, your teenager must commit to having ongoing and open discussions with you to sort out and think through new experiences.

 **ALERT!**

If your child is on an accelerated path through adolescence—because of early physical maturity or athletic or academic advancement—the most important component of effective discipline to have in place is open and honest and ongoing communication between the two of you.

Readjusting Expectations

Unless you understand that an adolescent is no longer a child, and how the two periods of growth can differ, you are likely to carry unrealistic expectations into your child's adolescence. These expectations can make parenting a teenager more emotionally difficult than it needs to be.

What You're Used To

Expectations are the connections that you create in your mind to anticipate change as you move from an old to a new situation, condition, or relationship. Expectations seek to answer the question, "What will the new reality be like?" When your expectations are met, and the new reality is the one that you've anticipated, you tend to feel okay about it, even if you don't like the changes. "Although having a child has changed our marriage, in a lot of ways being parents is working out pretty much how I thought it would." But when the reality is different from what you anticipated, the changes can be difficult to deal with emotionally.

 **FACT**

A lot of "discipline problems" in their child's adolescence are not discipline problems at all, but simply a case of parents' holding on to the unrealistic expectation that an adolescent would and should still act like a child.

There are three kinds of expectations that parents have grown used to their son's or daughter's meeting: predictions, ambitions, and conditions. One common prediction is, "Our child will follow our rules." When the child meets this prediction, parents feel in control and secure. One common ambition is, "We want our child to stay closely connected to family." When the child meets this ambition, parents feel attached and loved. One of their conditions is, "Our child should communicate directly and honestly with us." When the child meets this condition, parents feel informed and trustful. In each case, the reality parents expect in their child is the reality they encounter.

Changes

When positive expectations of their child are met, parents feel well and good. But what happens when, in the course of normal developmental change, the adolescent stops behaving exactly like he or she did as a child, yet parents cling to that old set of expectations? Now there can be an emotional price to pay.

For example, their child pushes against their limits, testing their rules, and the parents' old prediction that the child will obey doesn't hold up. This is not what parents expected. Now they may feel surprised, out of control, anxious, or worried.

Or the parents' old ambition that wants to keep the child closely connected with family is overturned when their adolescent begins to be more interested in spending time with friends and gaining social independence. This is not what parents expected. Now they may feel disappointed, out of touch, sad, or lonely.

Parents may also feel threatened when their adolescent begins to violate their old condition and lies to get around their rules to gain more freedom. The child's occasional deceit is not what the parent expected after a childhood in which they could expect the child to deal with them honestly and directly. Now they may feel betrayed, distrustful, angry, or suspicious.

When positive expectations are violated, there are usually negative emotional consequences to pay.

Expecting Exceptions

Their child's adolescence is complicated enough for parents without adding the additional burden of unrealistic expectations. Remember that expectations are not permission. In the previous examples, parents should expect, not necessarily accept, some disobedience, social disconnection, and lying as part of normal adolescence. "Expect" does not mean "accept"!

All "expect" means is that you as a parent must anticipate the possibility of these new behaviors in adolescence. Then, when and if they occur, you'll be able to avoid doubling up behavior problems with the child by adding your own emotional problems from feeling surprised, disappointed, or betrayed. Instead, because the adolescent's behavior was not unexpected, you can just focus on what the teenager needs to be doing differently—acting more obediently, staying more adequately connected with family, telling the truth.

 **ESSENTIAL**

To expect adolescent changes does not mean you accept them all. "Expect" means to keep your expectations current with the changing reality of your child's growth so you can provide necessary discipline when the unacceptable occurs without overreacting emotionally.

The Four Stages of Adolescence

To help you keep your expectations in line with the normal changes of adolescent growth, what follows is a brief description of the adolescent process, with common problems parents often encounter in each of the four stages along the way.

Early Adolescence

Early adolescence usually unfolds between ages nine and thirteen, and problems are characterized by these common changes. The adolescent:

- Develops a negative attitude.
- Shows increased dissatisfaction at being defined and treated as a child.
- Shows less interest in traditional childhood activities and more boredom and restlessness from not knowing what to do.
- Feels a new sense of grievance about unfair demands and limits that adults in life impose.
- Resists authority more, with questioning, arguing, delaying compliance, and ignoring normal home and school responsibilities.

- Experiments more to see what he or she can get away with, including such activities as shoplifting, vandalizing, prank calls, and the beginning of substance experimentation.

Midadolescence

Midadolescence usually unfolds between ages thirteen and fifteen, and problems are characterized by these common changes. The adolescent:

- Fights more with parents over social freedom.
- Lies more often to escape consequences from wrongdoing or to get to do what you have forbidden.
- Feels more peer pressure to go along with risk taking in order to belong, including more pressure to use illegal substances to be accepted.

Late Adolescence

Late adolescence usually unfolds between ages fifteen and eighteen, and problems are characterized by these common changes. The adolescent:

- Gains more independence by doing grown-up activities—part-time employment, driving a car, dating, and recreational substance use at social gatherings.
- Experiences more significant emotional (and often sexual) involvement in romantic relationships.
- Feels grief over the gradual separation from old friends (and perhaps leaving family) and more anxiety at his or her unreadiness to undertake more worldly independence.

Trial Independence

Trial independence usually unfolds between ages eighteen and twenty-three, and problems are characterized by these common changes. The adolescent struggling to be adult:

- Has lower self-esteem from a sense of incompetence, not being able to adequately support all the demands and keep all the commitments of adult responsibility at this "grown-up" age.
- Feels anxious over not having a clear sense of direction in life.
- Is easily distracted by peers who are confused about direction, too, partying more to deny problems or escape responsibility, as the period of maximum exposure to drug and alcohol use begins.

ESSENTIAL

Maintain realistic expectations about your child's passage through adolescence, and you will reduce the likelihood of overreacting when normal problems occur and helpful disciplinary support is required.

Substance Abuse

Like it or not, and most parents don't, you have to raise your child in a drug-filled world. From legal to illegal, from recreational to medicinal, from those in your bathroom cabinet to those in your cleaning closet or garage, from those in the drugstore to those sold on the street, mood- and mind-altering substances are everywhere to be found. The adolescent years are ripe for experimentation with these drugs.

So, what are you as parents supposed to do? Since you can't change the world, does that mean you are helpless to protect your son or daughter from the dangers of alcohol and drugs? No! There is a lot that you can do. You can't actually control your child's choices when it comes to alcohol and drug use, but you can definitely inform those choices with the best information and understanding you have. You can inform your child about the nature of the problem, about the risks involved, and about keeping oneself safe should the decision to use occur. And you can inform your-selves about signs to watch for that might indicate substance-related troubles in your child's life.

Signs of Substance Use to Watch For

It takes parental vigilance to help keep a child drug-free, so parents need to know what signs of substance use to watch for. There are general and specific indicators that are worth keeping an eye out for as your child makes the journey through adolescence.

 **FACT**

> According to a study by the American Psychological Association, 70 percent of high school students have tried cigarette smoking, 25 percent before the age of thirteen; 81 percent of high school students have tried alcohol, 32 percent having their first drink before the age of thirteen; and 47 percent of high school students have tried marijuana, 11 percent of which tried marijuana before the age of thirteen.

Some of the general indicators have to do with your teenager's making decisions that seem uncharacteristic or inconsistent with the established history and true character of the person as you know him or her to be. In each case, substance use takes the user from a caring to a noncaring (freedom from normal caring) mental frame of reference. Here are some common examples.

- A normally honest child starts lying.
- A normally smart child starts making unwise decisions.
- A normally motivated child starts becoming apathetic.
- A normally well-performing child starts failing.
- A normally obedient child starts getting into social trouble.
- A normally even-tempered child starts becoming explosive.
- A normally confiding child starts avoiding communication.
- A normally responsible child starts acting irresponsibly.

- A normally healthy child starts becoming run down.
- A normally constructive child starts acting self-destructively.

Always be on the lookout for atypical changes in your son or daughter as he or she journeys through adolescence. None of these general changes by themselves are sure signs of substance use, but three or four of them together should cause you to question if alcohol or drug use may be disorganizing your teenager's life.

There are also more specific indicators to be on the watch for. Here are some common behaviors to notice.

- You receive phone calls for your child where the caller refuses to give a name or the calling party just hangs up.
- You discover empty alcohol containers or drug paraphernalia in your child's room, backpack, or car.
- Your child is charged with minor in possession, possessing to sell, or driving while intoxicated.
- Money or pawnable items are stolen from family members.
- Your child is in possession of more money than you are providing.
- Your liquor supply is disappearing faster than you are drinking it, or it is watered down.
- There is a steady decline in your child's school attendance, a rise in disciplinary problems at school, and more rule breaking at home.
- Your child continually lies, and when confronted, lies about the lies.
- Every time you want to discuss the possibility of substance use with your child, he or she flies into a fury and refuses to talk about the subject.

If you see three or four of these indicators present in your child's life and he or she cannot give you a satisfactory explanation for these behaviors, you may want to take your son or daughter to a certified substance abuse counselor to assess if alcohol or drugs are playing a part in what is going on.

Coping with Teenage Substance Use

In their fear of the problem, parents often think punishment is the best deterrent to further use. It is not. To persuade yourself of this reality, just consider the high percentage of people in jail for drug or drug-related offenses. They are being punished, but how many of them come out and live drug-free? Not many.

The most significant way you can deal with this issue is communication. What might you communicate? Consider the following.

- **State your value position.** "You do not have our blessing to use alcohol or drugs. Should you choose to use, we will talk about that episode of use and we may decide some sanction shall follow."
- **Give a rational explanation against use.** "There are a lot of ways you can get hurt as you grow through adolescence. Substance use only increases these risks. We want you to follow a sober path because that is safest."
- **Offer to share your personal and current history with alcohol and drug use.** "I would like to give you the benefit of what alcohol and drug experience I have had so you can learn from what I've learned, from dangers I've seen, and from mistakes I've made. In return, I would like you to share your exposure to substances with me so I can help you learn from the experience."
- **Share any history of substance use problems in the immediate and extended family.** "Here are some cautionary stories about how substance use has caused problems for some of the people in our family system that you know. Perhaps hearing about choices they made can inform choices that you make."
- **Declare the topic of substances and substance use a topic always open for family discussion.** "It is important for us to talk about alcohol and drugs as they indirectly or directly affect your experience—from what you hear, from what you see, and from what you may decide to do. Of course, if

you ever have any questions or concerns about my substance use, like alcohol, I'm open to discussing that."

- **Give your child a double message.** "We don't want you to use. But if the time comes when you choose to use, here are some ways to do it as safely as possible. For example, when it comes to alcohol, limit your drinking to beer, and to no more than two beers a night. Don't mix drinking beer with any other kinds of alcohol or other substances. Don't drink to keep up with other people's drinking. Don't get into drinking competitions over who can drink the most. Don't drink to get drunk. Don't drive if you drink. Don't be driven by someone else who's been drinking. Call me anytime if you need a safe ride home."

Get Help

If the warning signs have led to your assessment that your teenager is using alcohol to intentional excess (drinking to get drunk) or using other drugs that in a wide variety of ways are creating dangerous risk-taking or causing physical harm, then you must take protective action. In either case, if your child shows signs of abuse (no longer caring about what has traditionally mattered and making self-destructive choices), or signs of addiction (becoming dependent on substances and being unable to stop), then you must take protective action. When your child shows signs of intentional excess, abuse, or addiction, get a qualified drug abuse counselor to assess your teenager's substance use. It will help confirm or disconfirm your suspicions, it will show your child that you are seriously concerned about the possibility of harmful substance use in his or her life, and it will open the door to some level of treatment if that is advised.

If a substance problem is confirmed, no matter what treatment help may be sought at this time, parents need to assert strong and supportive discipline at home by taking a restrictive stand that essentially reduces freedoms and imposes demands to encourage the re-establishment of healthy, responsible drug-free behavior in their child. The teen can earn back his freedom as he meets the demands you set.

What kinds of conditions for healthy and responsible family living do parents typically impose? Here are a few.

- There will be zero tolerance for alcohol and drug use.
- There will be random drug testing.
- There will be no discretionary money.
- There will be no driving unless to school and back and to work and back, subject to parental supervision.
- There will be no going to parties and all socializing will be subject to parental approval.
- Any paychecks from employment will be turned over to parents for approved spending, agreed-upon saving, and making restitution for any thefts or damages that substance-using behavior has caused.
- All household rules will be followed and all family activities will require cheerful participation.
- Investment of regular time and energy in positive personal growth activities will be made.

 **ALERT!**

Don't enable your substance-abusing teenager by solving his or her problems, giving second chances, or rescuing from consequences. The more you "help" in these ways, the more power of self-help you encourage the child to give up, the more learning from experience you prevent. Attend Al-Anon meetings yourself for support and guidance.

As these and other conditions for personal conduct are met, as the teenager shows evidence of living in more constructive, drug-free ways, this good behavior will be rewarded with more freedom and independence. Finally, remember that the surest way to raise "drug-free" children is to be drug-free parents—either using in moderation with no problems in their own or other people's eyes, or simply not using at all.

The Freedom Contract

The entire ten- to twelve-year process of adolescence is fraught with risks. Your child will be trying out many experiences for the first time, he'll be exposed to more worldly influences than ever before, and he will generally be unappreciative of the demands and limits of responsibility that you are striving to teach.

Frustrated by your refusal to grant permission, your adolescent may complain, "You never let me do anything! Everyone else has more freedom than I do! You just don't want me to grow up!" Not so. What you want is for your son or daughter to grow up without falling prey to dangerous exposures and damaging choices. This is why, at the outset of adolescence (by ages nine to ten), you must make it very clear that, when it comes to granting more freedom, you intend to hold your child to the freedom contract.

QUESTION?

How do I know it's time to enter into a freedom contract with my child?
When he or she starts pushing for more independent choice and more social freedom of experience away from home, you need to specify your terms of permission.

What do you need from your teenager when he or she wants permission for more freedom from you? You want evidence that your adolescent is trustworthy in six distinct ways. Together they add up to form the "freedom contract," stipulating conditions that your teenager must meet before you agree to risk allowing more discretionary choices. The six provisions are:

- "You will keep us reasonably informed by giving us adequate and accurate information about what is going on in your life and what you are planning to do."
- "You will live in a two-way relationship with us, doing for

us in fair exchange for our doing for you, contributing to the family as the family contributes to you."

- "You will honor your word, keeping agreements and following through on commitments you make with us."
- "Your conduct will be your passport to permission by showing us responsible behavior at home, at school, and out in the world."
- "You will be available for a free and open discussion of any concern we may need to discuss."
- "You will communicate to us with respect, fulfilling agreements with a positive attitude, acting gladly and not angrily in response to our requests and restraints."

When your teenager wants to negotiate more freedom—such as a later curfew, permission to date, or getting a driver's license—she knows that she must meet these six provisions first. This means demonstrating by actions, not just in words. You are not interested in promises. You are accepting only evidence of performance. Promises have no bargaining power.

ESSENTIAL

If parents want their child to live up to the freedom contract, then they need to honor those six provisions as well. Live up to the standards of responsibility to which you hold your child.

At such negotiation points, if your teenager has shown evidence of being truthful, being helpful, keeping agreements, acting responsibly, being open to discussion, and talking respectfully, then you tend to be more inclined to consent with his or her request.

If, however, your teenager has not been living up to the contract (lying to you, taking but not giving, breaking agreements, acting irresponsibly, refusing to discuss concerns with you, or communicating disrespectfully), then you may be inclined to deny the request. You may even reduce existing freedom for a while until the provisions of the freedom contract begin to be honored once again.

This is the basis for discipline during the adolescent years. The next chapters will cover in more detail some of the specific problems you may encounter in each stage of adolescence.

CHAPTER 17

Early Adolescence
(Ages 9–13)

I T TAKES COURAGE FOR YOUR CHILD to begin the process of adolescence, pushing against and pulling away from your control to gain more independence from family and freedom for self-determination, letting his or her "bad" (more abrasive) side out, arousing some degree of your disapproval in the process.

It also takes courage for you to parent your child through adolescence, taking stands for the boy's or girl's best interests against what he or she may want, letting your "boss" (more authoritarian) side out, arousing some disapproval from your child in the process.

With the onset of adolescence, the hard "half" of parenting begins. Now you face the challenge of keeping up loving closeness and discipline with your son or daughter as more social separation and conflict over differences are helping you to start growing apart.

Signs of Early Adolescence

Although parents commonly identify adolescence with the "teenage" years, early adolescence actually begins before that. Usually unfolding between the ages of nine and thirteen, it starts in elementary school. Although the second-grade teacher may describe most of the class as usually serious, focused, calm, good-humored, curious, industrious, attentive, enthusiastic, positive, cooperative, and friendly; the fifth-grade teacher may describe more of the class as often silly, disorganized, restless, moody, disinterested, indolent, distracted, apathetic, negative, resistant, and even hostile. So don't take a lot of early adolescent changes personally. Your son or daughter is not only more difficult to parent, but also more difficult to teach. You're not the only adult who is contending with this transformation. And your child is not the only one growing through this change.

 **FACT**

A sure sign that your child has entered adolescence is when you have become a social embarrassment to your son or daughter in public. The first grader responds to your surprise classroom visit with delight, but the same surprise mortifies your fifth grader.

Your Child's Changing Behavior

If you had unquestioned authority in childhood, you will have more questioned authority in early adolescence. If you were your child's preferred company before, you will come second to the company of his or her friends now. If you were the object of appreciation before, you will receive more complaints and criticism now. Parents who take these changes personally and feel disrespected, rejected, or otherwise devalued often want to pull away or even be negative in return. "Well if that's the way you're going to act, I don't want anything to do with you!" This is a mistake.

From here on out, your child needs you more than ever for the constancy of your caring, for the influence of your communication, and for the stability of your support. Thus, if you are a parent who had a "best friend" relationship with your child, always confiding in each other and doing things together, and now has an early adolescent who wants to talk less and disclose less to you than before, don't cut off conversation or invitations to companionship. Keep initiating opportunities to talk, keep the door open to communication so your child has a continuing chance to talk with you when he or she feels willing and able. Keep asking your child to do things with you, and don't let refusals keep you from continuing to extend these invitations. Don't treat normal adolescent separation as rejection.

Signs of Closeness

Remember, separating from childhood is also painful for your son or daughter. He or she doesn't want to be treated and defined as a child anymore but still misses a lot of the closeness that went with those early years. For example, no longer willing to snuggle up against you on the couch or be kissed because he feels too grown up for these old shows of affection, your eleven-year-old allows (and needs) a sideways hug and an "I love you," both of which he can still accept. To be treated "as a child" feels embarrassing; but to be denied all expressions of parental affection that went with "being a child" feels isolating.

 **ESSENTIAL**

Do not grow out of "touch," literally, with your adolescent. Feeling too grown up to accept being hugged and kissed by you, your early adolescent will still accept a friendly pat on the shoulder that physically expresses your loving care.

Insecurity and Low Self-Esteem

Change is scary for your early adolescent, knowing he or she is becoming transformed, but to what effect? Consider some of the levels on which your child is beginning to change.

Physical Changes

Physically there is the feeling of being helpless over one's body, particularly if puberty has started to release estrogen and testosterone. Now the child becomes self-conscious about body hair and body odor, the girl contending with growing breasts and menstruation, the boy seeing his testicles enlarge and having wet dreams, both children careening through growth spurts over which they have no power.

And if puberty has not begun for them but has for others, that becomes cause for concern. "When will I start looking more grown up?" Each morning there is the excruciating encounter with the mirror, examining oneself pore by pore to see what awful change has befallen one's body overnight that must be taken to school for everyone to see, for everyone to make fun of. "Look at her!" "Look at him!"

The early adolescent truly believes that other people will be as merciless in their scrutiny as the adolescent is with him- or herself. So, the adolescent explodes in anger at her parents, who are trying to be reassuring about her appearance: "Don't tell me I look nice. I know how awful I look!"

He or she also has concerns about developing sexually too fast or not developing at all. Now all the complexity and confusion about how to define one's sexual gender begins. "How am I supposed to look and act? To what degree do I fit the advertised ideal?" What is womanly and what is manly and how does the early adolescent begin to achieve one of those definitions?

ALERT!

Personal insecurity created by developmental change can cause early adolescents to engage in social cruelty by ganging up. A social bully intimidates a social victim, with followers collaborating in mistreatment that they fear receiving themselves. Bullies can learn to coerce, followers can learn to act cowardly, and victims can learn to be helpless. Make sure your child plays no role in this mean game.

Emotional Changes

Emotionally, the world becomes a dark, dramatic, and dangerous place to live, as poetry written and artwork created at this age amply testifies. The early adolescent lives in fear of, and fascination with, the harsh and violent side of the outside world he or she is about to begin exploring.

Then there are intense mood swings, with more extreme lows than highs, which seem unpredictable and inexplicable. "What's going on?" ask concerned parents. "Are you crazy, up one minute and down the next?" Thinks the adolescent, "Maybe that's it; maybe I'm going crazy!"

Social Changes

Socially, the world of peers (most of whom are beset by similar insecurity) has become extremely competitive, conniving, and cruel, as friends vie with each other for group membership and popularity. Relationships become extremely unstable. Yesterday's best friend may not speak to your child tomorrow. Rumoring and gossip, teasing and bullying, rejecting and excluding are all part of the social harshness of the age. "How do I fit in; who are my real friends?"

Academically, concentration on schoolwork is broken by concern over all these other developmental changes. It's hard to keep one's mind on studying when it feels like one's physical, emotional, and daily social survival is at stake. "It's much harder to do well in school than it was before!"

Beset by personal doubt and the delusion of uniqueness, your child at this age makes an unhappy comparison: "No one else feels the way I do!" He or she then proceeds to the question that most early adolescents wonder at some point: "What's the matter with me?" The answer is usually a list of indictments provided by his or her worst fears: "I'm stupid, I'm ugly, I'm a loser, I have no friends."

Your Approach to Discipline

It is worthwhile for you to keep this portrait of early adolescence in mind when it comes to disciplining your child at this very vulnerable age. In general, nonevaluative correction needs to be the order of the day. "We disagree with the choice you have made, this is why, and here is what you need to do in consequence." No personal criticism allowed. Your early adolescent is already too down on herself for her own good.

ALERT!

> If your early adolescent has a teacher who uses public put-downs to keep students in their place, meet with the teacher to affirm your support for classroom order and to express concern about the use of sarcasm as a classroom management technique.

Most important, do not put your early adolescent down with teasing, humor, or sarcasm. Being laughed at, being made fun of, being ridiculed, and being made to look foolish all lead to the most painful emotional state at this age: embarrassment. And although embarrassment may seem a slight discomfort for you, it is one small step from shame for the early adolescent. Children take special handling at this painfully self-conscious and insecure age. You don't want to make a hard passage worse.

Separation from Childhood

Early adolescence begins the separation from childhood. The child, through words and actions, begins to differentiate himself from the child he used to be. This differentiation is commonly expressed in four ways.

- "I am different from how I was as a child," your son or daughter seems to say, and now rejects much of what used to be valued, while trying on new images, interests, activities, and associations.
- "I want to be treated differently than I was as a child," your son or daughter seems to say, and now demands less traditional restraints and more independent freedom.

- "I am becoming different from how you are," your son or daughter seems to say, and now develops new cultural tastes and identifications that are counter to those you have traditionally held, that fit less well into the family.
- "I am going to act differently than you want me to behave," your son or daughter seems to say, and now your rules are questioned, response to your requests is delayed, and your authority is more contested by complaint and argument.

Increased Resistance

Each type of "different" statement, each time it is made, is a statement of separation. And when you have reached your tolerance limits for this differentiation and draw the line ("I will not allow that kind of poster on your bedroom walls!"), your child will, at the least, show resentment and will most likely raise conflict over it. From now on, you will be parenting against more resistance as your early adolescent pushes to create more room to grow. Your son or daughter will feel he or she fits less well into the family than in his or her childhood. To some degree, both parents and early adolescent will become more uncomfortable with each other as differentiation occurs.

You are both redrawing the boundaries of definition, which will result in some degree of compromise between you. Your early adolescent will not get freedom to act as completely different as he or she would like, and you will come to tolerate more different behavior in your son or daughter than you ever thought you would.

More Corrective Discipline

In this process of separation, particularly if your son or daughter was mostly on good behavior in childhood, it can feel that the boy or girl is now letting his or her "bad side" out. "Bad" doesn't mean evil, immoral, or unlawful. It means becoming more resistant, oppositional, and abrasive to live with.

In response, parents usually become more corrective in order to keep the early adolescent in line. By becoming more corrective, parents are now seen as not as "nice" to live with and seem "meaner." This is a necessary change in the relationship. For a child to justify early adolescent changes that go with letting the bad side out, it helps if they see parents as letting their bad (corrective) side out, too. "If you can be harder to live with," the early adolescent seems to say, "then so can I."

 **FACT**

Teenagers are naturally offensive. A healthy teenager pushes for maximum freedom to grow as soon as he or she can get it. Healthy parents restrain that push out of concerns for safety and responsibility. This is the healthy conflict of opposing interests that unfolds over the course of adolescence.

A Sign It's Working

There is, however, one critical distinction you want your son or daughter at this age to be able to make. You'll know your child has made this distinction when your adult friends compliment you on how well behaved your early adolescent is in their presence. "You can't be describing our child!" you protest, knowing how difficult your relationship with him or her at home can sometimes be. But the eyes of the world don't lie. Your early adolescent has enough common social sense to understand not to treat outside adults the way he or she sometimes treats you.

Your child is doing what you want him to: showing his good side out in the world and letting his bad side out only with you at home, reserving it for the adults whom he trusts to keep loving him no matter how resistant his behavior. Since every adolescent needs room to express both good side and bad, you'd rather the bad was confined to home while the good was shown to the outside world.

The Negative Attitude

One of the first signs of early adolescence is what parents often describe as "the bad attitude." They can't understand it. Here is a child who used to be so positive about life, so enthusiastic, and now it's like someone has pulled the plug and all that positive energy has been drained away. Now the child just lies around, frustrated and bored and restless, complaining about having "nothing to do." But no matter what suggestion you make for an activity, you are told that your idea is a bad one and that you just don't understand. So then you decide that since your child doesn't know what to do, and there is plenty of work to be done around the place, maybe what you need to do is put that large, capable body to work. "Not now! Leave me alone! Can't you see I'm tired?" comes the offended response. Then the phone rings, and suddenly there's plenty of energy to go hang out with a friend.

Now negative energy begins to build. As a child, your daughter probably accepted that her personal freedom depended on your permission, and more often than not, that was okay with her. Now, however, with childhood closing down and the exciting grown-up world opening up, your limits and demands are becoming a major grievance. "What do you mean you won't let me? That's not fair! Who gave you the right to tell me what I can and cannot do? You're not the boss of the world!" But you are the boss of the early adolescent's world, and now she doesn't like it. It is this negativity caused by the loss of old enthusiasms and the onset of new grievances, that creates the negative attitude.

The negative attitude begins the process of adolescence. People do not want to personally change unless they are dissatisfied with who and how they are. Now the early adolescent wants a change. He or she doesn't want to be defined and treated as a "child" anymore. Early adolescence can coincide with the onset of puberty, but it doesn't have to. When it does, early adolescence is considerably more intense. But the primary motivator for early adolescence is the dissatisfaction generated by the negative attitude.

Two common disciplinary problems created for parents at the negative attitude phase of early adolescence are taking negativity out on others and throwing away childish things.

Taking Negativity out on Others

No wonder your early adolescent feels negative. She's rejecting the idea of being a child and the interests and attachments that went with it, and doesn't yet have anything positive to replace the loss, so her self-esteem drops. More in life seems to be going wrong than right. So, after a socially difficult day at school, your eleven-year-old comes home brimming with negativity, immediately picking on a younger brother or sister, driving the child to tears, just to take out bad feelings on someone else. Now negativity about self has turned into meanness toward others, just as it does in peer relationships at school at this age.

 **FACT**

Because the early adolescent wants more independence but still wants to be taken care of, parents can get mixed messages at this confused and confusing age. "Leave me alone; keep me company." "Let me do it; do it for me." "Don't make me come; don't leave me behind."

Trying to feel better by trying to make others feel worse, however, is not an acceptable way for your early adolescent to manage negativity. Therefore, you need to confront, discourage, and redirect this behavior. "It is perfectly all right for you to get down about your life, but it is not okay to act those unhappy feelings out on others. I'd like you to talk them out instead. Please know that whenever you have a down mood or a bad day, I am always willing to listen, and to help you find a way to feel better if that is what you'd like. But using others as your whipping post at home is not allowed."

Throwing Away Childish Things

In the spirit of rejecting the childish part of himself or herself to declare independence from childhood, your early adolescent may want to quit an activity that has historically been an important source of self-esteem. Since you want your son or daughter to have as many pillars of self-esteem as possible, to give one up at this fragile time does not seem like a good idea. Rather than get into an argument about whose activity it is, however, and who should have the right to make the decision, be willing to consider quitting on condition that the boy or girl agree to a delay. "Let's both think about it for three months. If at the end of that time you still want to give up the sport, we will talk seriously about it. In the meantime, think about all the ways you have enjoyed it—from the pleasure of playing to the company of friends."

During this transition, you may have to put up with a hard compromise. Every practice, your son or daughter complains about going, you insist, there is an argument, you still insist, the boy or girl grudgingly gives consent, and once at practice he or she has a good time. This is the compromise: He or she gets to protest going there, you get blamed for causing a "childish" activity to be continued, and the early adolescent is then free to continue an old activity that can still be enjoyed because you "made" him or her go.

Finally, at the end of the period you've agreed on, if your son or daughter still wants to give up the activity, then agree by imposing another condition. "If you really want to give up this activity, that is okay with me so long as you substitute a similar activity we both agree on in its place." You want a new support of self-esteem to replace the old.

Rebellion

People do not rebel without a reason, and the early adolescent finds just cause for rebellion: what he sees as the infringement of personal freedom. It feels unfair to be made to do what he or she doesn't want to do, and to be kept from doing what he or she does want to do. Basic rights of self-determination are being denied by the powers that be at home, at school, and out in the world. What is the early adolescent to do?

The answer is rebel. Actively and passively, your son or daughter becomes more resistant to your demands and restraints, creating two common disciplinary problems for you to deal with—automatic arguments and endless delays.

Automatic Arguments

A negative attitude gives the adolescent the motivation to change, and rebellion gives him the *power* to change. Standing up to parental authority by questioning their demands is one way this is done. Parents who have a low tolerance for argument are often at high risk of overreacting when arguments occur. "Don't you talk back to me!"

Rather than empowering the early adolescent when he or she attempts to argue with you, remember that it takes two to make an argument. Your son or daughter can't argue with you unless you agree to argue back. So when your request is greeted with a challenge back, "Why should I have to do what you say?" declare your unwillingness to argue and repeat your insistence on what you have asked. "As I said, this is what I need to have you do."

 **ALERT!**

Because standing up to parents by arguing takes courage, never purposely or nervously smile or laugh during this exchange. Feeling ridiculed and humiliated, your adolescent will get very angry at you for taking lightly what he or she means seriously and is brave to do.

But before you write off all arguments as being irritating and unproductive, appreciate the plus side of what your son or daughter is doing. He or she is daring to speak up to your authority, is learning how to state his or her position, is willing to argue his or her case against more skilled opposition, is secure enough to brave your disapproval, and is tough enough to refuse you automatic or immediate obedience. Children who are willing to stand up to parents are usually willing to stand up to peers and the pressure to conform that they can create. Children who automatically do what their parents ask without any resistance often may be at higher risk of doing what they are told by dominating friends (not to mention dangerous strangers).

Arguing is active resistance. It is about learning to stand up for oneself. And before children learn to do it with peers, they must learn to do it with parents.

However, don't ever agree to argue about what you have no intention to change. The more your son or daughter argues, the more invested in persuading you he or she becomes, the more angry he or she gets on finding out that your mind was made up from the beginning.

Endless Delay

So you have asked your early adolescent one, two, three, four times to do the dishes and they are still not done. Every time you agree to "wait a minute," you end up waiting another twenty. So finally, in exasperation, you raise your voice and command, "I want them done now!" Whereupon your son or daughter looks at you and in a disapproving voice declares, "Well, you don't have to get so upset about it!" So the dishes finally get washed. But not with soap. So you are back to square one.

What's going on? Passive resistance is the power of delay. It's a compromise. In actions, the early adolescent is saying, "You can tell me what, I'll tell you when, and when I get enough 'when,' I'll do what you want—partly." The best way to deal with endless delay is with relentless insistence (supervision), either using nagging to wear down your child's passive resistance, or waiting until the next exchange point to get your request met.

Do not give additional power to this passive resistance by getting upset, by backing off your request, or (worst of all) by fulfilling the request yourself. If it's worth asking your child to do, then it is definitely worth not defaulting on your request and doing it yourself.

Not only will you let your son or daughter win with passive resistance, but you will end up feeling angry at doing what someone else should have done.

Both active and passive resistance work to some degree. The early adolescent does gain more power of self-determination than she had before because no parents can hold out against this resistance all the time. It's the end of the day. You're just human. You're tired. You don't want an argument, you're too weary to pursue delay, so you just let some of your requests go. And every time you do, your son or daughter gathers a little more power, which sets the stage for the last phase of early adolescence—early experimentation.

Early Experimentation

With freedom gained from both active and passive resistance, your son or daughter is now curious to experience the world beyond childhood and to see what illicit freedoms he or she can get away with. At this phase, both you and your child are asking the same question, but you each have very different viewpoints attached to what you want to know. The common question is, "What if?" For you, this is a worry question: "What if my child tried something dangerous and got hurt?" For your early adolescent, this is an excitement question: "What if I tried something scary to see what it was like?" You want to prevent the risks your son or daughter wants to take. Where he or she sees the possibility for adventure, you see the potential for harm.

 **ESSENTIAL**

> Remember, you're not out to change your child's mind; you're out to add your own, more mature perspective.

But when, for example, you share your concerns about the dangers of experimenting with substances at this age (a time when trying cigarettes and inhalants often begins), your early adolescent either denies any interest or denies that it can cause the harm you say it can. "I've got friends who do it some, and they say they don't get hurt."

When it comes to a lot of early substance experimentation, you can't actually control your child's choice, but you can definitely inform it, and you should. Weigh in with an adult perspective to counter the untruths that your child's peers are all too willing to share. "Your aunt, my sister, smoked cigarettes and got lung cancer. So when your friends tell you smoking is safe, you need to know they are mistaken."

All growth requires taking risks, and all risk taking is enabled by denial: "Bad things won't happen to me because I'm too smart and I'll be careful." What is frustrating for parents is trying to argue this with denial. So don't do it. Denial is part of this experimental age. Accept it. And then feel free to speak up with all of your concerns about various kinds of risk taking so your son or daughter can enter what you have to say into what they decide to think.

Early experimentation is about gathering the experience needed to change. To this end, your adolescent's interest in seeing what he or she can get away with can cause a major set of discipline problems, all involving testing limits, at this time.

Testing Limits

Testing limits should be treated seriously and not discounted by parents who just chalk it up to "innocent mischief." Let "small" violations go and larger ones will follow. If you don't take your stands for acceptable behavior early, it may soon prove too late.

Three common kinds of limit testing at this age are prank calling, vandalizing, and shoplifting. In each case, your early adolescent, usually in the company of friends, victimizes someone. When he and his friends make a threatening late-night prank call to the old man down the block, they think it's fun to hear his frightened response. When they spray paint the outside of the school, they think it's cool to leave their mark on a public place. When they take items from a store, they think they've beaten the system by getting goods cost-free.

In each case, they're testing social limits to see if they are real, to see if they will hold. As parents, your job is to show your son or daughter that when you break a social limit and are caught, you pay a social price. Your job is to close the loop of responsibility on these occasions.

Closing the Loop of Responsibility

For every major violation, a consequence will follow—that's the law of enforcement parents have to mandate at this early experimental age. Confrontation with the victim, responding to the victim, and restitution to the victim must all occur. Of these consequences, the first is the one your son or daughter will dread the most. He has to face the old man he prank called and listen to him tell what it felt like to receive a threatening call. She has to face the principal and listen as she describes what it is like to have the school defaced. He has to face the store manager and listen to her say what it was like to be stolen from. This is how the loop of responsibility begins to be closed.

Next, the boy or girl has to respond to what he or she has heard in a way that recognizes the hurt that he or she has inflicted. And finally, some form of restitution to the injured party must be made. By connecting bad choice with unwelcome consequence, parents encourage the early adolescent to rethink testing limits and learn a lesson of responsibility from his or her misdeed.

Now you know what to expect as adolescence begins. Next up: midadolescence, which brings a whole host of new disciplinary issues to confront.

CHAPTER 18

Midadolescence (Ages 13-15)

IF THERE IS ONE STAGE of adolescence where maximum conflict between parents and teenager is likely to occur, it is midadolescence. Now, disagreement over freedom is no longer about a theoretical matter of principle, as it was in early adolescence. It has become intensely practical. The teenager begins to contest to what degree you can actually restrict the freedom he or she wants. "You can't make me, and you can't stop me! You're running a home, not a prison, you know!"

Your Adolescent's Worldview

Of course, on one level, your teenager is correct, but on another, he's running a bluff. You may not have direct control over his choices, but you have plenty of indirect influence: his attachment to you, your persuasive techniques, the importance of your approval, the power of your authority, and his dependence on you in a host of material ways.

The Push for Freedom

The push for freedom at this age can be extremely strong, driven by your teenager's frantic need to be out in the world in the company of friends, doing what they want to do. "If I can't be with them, I won't belong!" It feels like there is no time but the present, and the teenager will mortgage the future to free up the present by promising anything later for freedom now. "I'll stay home the whole next month if I can just go to the party tonight!"

Conflicts over timing plague the relationship between parents and midadolescent. The teenager feels like she will "die," feels like her life will be "ruined," if you refuse her the freedom that her friends are allowed.

ALERT!

When you are having doubts about consenting to a request from your midadolescent for more freedom, stall so that you have time to think it through. Question for information, check the arrangements, push to get your demands for safety met, and say no if you don't feel comfortable saying yes.

The Tyranny of Now

Now is all that matters to the midadolescent, whereas parents are trying to slow down deliberation by considering how pleasure now might lead to risks or problems later. To this end, parents want time to think—to gather more information, assess risks, consider safety, and require assurances. Although the teenager doesn't mind delaying on parental requests, having parents delay on a teenager's request feels intolerable to her. So as parents, you have to hang tough: "If you are saying you have to know right now whether you can go and it's now or never, then our answer is 'never,' because you have to give us time to think through your request."

Social Extortion

So now the teenager ups the pressure on the next request by adding social extortion to the urgency of getting a decision now. In front of a group of impatiently waiting friends, who apparently have already received parental permission, your teenager asks if she, too, can go. Your teenager is banking on your saying yes to spare her the social embarrassment of refusing her request in front of her friends.

Instead, you say that you and she will have to talk about this alone in the next room, and her friends can either wait for your decision or go without her. And now your teenager is embarrassed. "How could you treat me like that, like a little child, with all of them standing there?" Then you explain, "I won't be pressured or trapped into making any quick decisions by being put on the spot in front of your friends."

The Game of Loopholes

To get desired freedom, the midadolescent will often become deceptive. He or she may play a constant game of looking for loopholes, looking for running room where no parental rule or prohibition has been put into place. After the fact, parents find themselves plugging openings the best they can.

"Well, you never said I couldn't!" innocently protests the teenager as though he didn't know "borrowing" your credit card was against any rules and considered wrong. Catching up with the unforeseen infraction, the parent replies, "Because I never thought you would! But since you have, you need to know that borrowing without permission is stealing. You can't do that in this family, and you will pay me back!"

 **FACT**

Taking stronger stands against your teenager's stronger wants for social freedom during midadolescence will create more conflict during this typically stormy time. When conflict occurs, be sure to model, and insist on, the quality of communication you want in return.

Decoding Common Communications

Now, parents can misunderstand the teenager unless they can separate what their child actually means from what he's saying.

- "I can't help it" can mean "I won't stop it."
- "I don't know" can mean "I don't want you to know."
- "You don't understand" can mean "I don't want you to understand."
- "I forgot" can mean "I decided not to remember."
- "You don't trust me" can mean "You won't let me!"
- "I hate you" can mean "I am extremely angry at you."
- "You don't love me" can mean "You won't let me have my way."
- "I don't care" can mean "I care too much to let you know how much I care."
- "Well, it's not my fault" can mean "It is my fault, but I don't want to admit it."

Strains on the Relationship

The negative attitude, rebellion, and early experimentation of early adolescence take a psychological toll on the relationship between you and your son or daughter. The old parent/child relationship has been transformed in some predictable ways. The closeness you used to feel has given way to more distance. There are more disagreements to bridge than there used to be. You feel more dissatisfied with each other, former contentment giving way to more criticism on both sides. Greater distrust between you leads to more questioning—from you for more information about what's going on, from your teenager for more justification of your rules and decisions. All the while, increasing differences are creating more intolerance between you in place of the mutual acceptance that was the order of the day in childhood.

By midadolescence, parent and teenager may have a more disaffected relationship. Each side develops a list of common complaints against the other. Parents will often charge, "You're too young to understand, too adventurous, too untrustworthy, too uncommunicative, too unhelpful, too messy, too irritating, too unconcerned with family, too unreliable, and too interested in bad music." Teenagers will often charge in return, "Well, you're too old to understand, too protective, too untrusting, too prying, too demanding, too fussy, too easily upset, too concerned with family, too controlling, and too ignorant of good music."

ALERT!

Under no circumstances should you tell your teenager that he or she is "only going through a phase." This is a dismissive statement. It is insulting. You wouldn't tell someone struggling with the infirmities of aging that he or she is "only going through a phase."

When these complaints rule the relationship, a healthy mutual dislike can sometimes develop between the parents, who won't stop insisting on responsibility, and the teenager, who won't stop pushing for freedom. To keep this dislike from becoming unhealthy, keep a larger positive perspective and do not use hurtful language or say hurtful things.

The Shell of Self-Centeredness

Midadolescence tends to encapsulate the teenager in three major concerns—with self, with fun, and with now. There is nothing wrong with any of these preoccupations. However, as responsible parents, you don't want these to be the sole concerns that govern your teen's behavior. Just because this shell of self-centeredness is normal at this age doesn't make it okay. To let it go unchallenged would do a disservice to you and your teenager. He or she would become hard to live with happily at home and would have a hard time getting along with others out in the world.

Your job is to try and penetrate this shell of self-centeredness with a disciplinary response, training your teenager to focus on additional concerns as well. To this end, in words and actions, you communicate as follows.

- "It's fine to focus on yourself, but you also have to think of others and consider their needs."
- "It's fine to want to have fun, but sometimes you have to work before you have fun or instead of having fun."
- "It's fine to want what you want right now, but sometimes you have to delay gratification or even do without."

During the midadolescent passage, you are responsible for helping your child learn this healthy mix—of self and other, of fun and work, of now and later—so he or she can put it into practice with others when away from home.

Avoiding Responsibility

At some point in midadolescence, most teenagers will choose to break the rules for freedom's sake, and when they get caught, they will try to escape responsibility for whatever they have done. They fear being held accountable for doing wrong and, as a consequence, having to pay the worst price of all—giving up some precious freedom to pay for what they've done.

So, confronted by parents about this misconduct, the teenager typically resorts to four defenses against admitting responsibility.

- He or she may lie to get out of trouble: "The policeman was mistaken. It was another guy, not me."
- He or she may blame others: "She drove away without paying, I was just a passenger."
- He or she may make excuses: "I was so tired from staying up late and studying for exams, I just wasn't thinking clearly about what I was doing."
- He or she may deny anything happened: "I don't know what you're talking about!"

When your child tries to use these escapes from responsibility, you must hold your teenager accountable for owning the decisions he made and the trouble that followed. Defenses against responsibility, like lying, blaming, excusing, and denying, are not only unacceptable, but they should be considered additional violations themselves and dealt with accordingly.

 **FACT**

> Getting your teenager to converse can be tricky. Asking can discourage your teen from communication, because now questions are emblematic of authority and invasive of privacy. Instead, model the sharing you want by sharing about yourself, and be accessible anytime she "feels like" talking.

You expect your adolescent to admit the truth and take ownership of her actions. You want to close the loop of responsibility for the present violation, and even more important, you want to provide training for the future. Don't allow these defenses to stand and let your teenager proceed through life believing that any time he or she makes a wrong choice and faces a bad consequence, escaping responsibility is okay to do. One goal of discipline is training your teenager to conduct his or her life in an accountable manner.

The Battle Against Authority

At a time when your teenager acts like your imposition of family demands, rules, and restraints is unwanted, unneeded, oppressive, and intolerable, you must keep that family structure firmly in place for his or her well-being and protection. At this age your teenager is excited and frightened by the same understanding about personal freedom: "You can't make me and you can't stop me!"

Although your teenager is correct, and although he or she argues the point at every opportunity, you will mostly be given consent because there is security in the structure you provide, and your son or daughter knows that. "But is it worth all the conflict?" some weary parents ask. The answer is definitely yes. Your midadolescent needs to fight against you to save face in order to go along with you to keep safe.

Understanding the combative nature of the consent you are often given at this age, you typically enforce structure in five ways.

- You make demands. ("This is what you need to do.")
- You set limits. ("This is what you can't do.")
- You allow or apply consequences. ("Because you did that, you must now do this.")
- You raise questions. ("Why did this happen?")
- You confront significant issues. ("We need to talk about your conduct last night.")

In midadolescence, a teenager will sometimes "go on a run." Intoxicated with freedom he or she is rebelliously unable to resist, the adolescent will break all curfew requirements in a headlong run toward excitement, danger, and the forbidden, usually in the company of like-minded friends. In this extreme case, what are parents supposed to do? Just give up, accept the situation, and act hopeless? No. Every time your teenager breaks the rules and leaves at this age, your job is to go after him or her, bring your son or daughter home, and reassert healthy rules around the child once again to create the opportunity for consent.

 **FACT**

Substance abuse makes midadolescent disciplinary issues more intense. It becomes harder for you to penetrate the shell of self-centeredness. The teen uses the defenses against responsibility more frequently. His or her resistance to your authority becomes more deeply entrenched.

"But she just sneaks out again!" Then you must go after her again. Going after her, bringing her home, reasserting healthy family rules, all show that you are actively there, that you care, and that wherever she runs, your parenting follows. In addition, you may want to seek the help of supplemental social authority. "If we set a boundary and you keep going beyond it, beyond where we can reach to restrain you, we will find someone who can. We will file a runaway report with the police and they, too, will be looking for you."

Communicating with Your Teen

Because the midadolescent is preoccupied with personal wants, social friendships, and worldly freedoms, it becomes significantly harder for parents to get the teenager's attention than it used to be. Parents have to be more persistent with their message, and when the message does get through, it is often not well received. Protective busyness ("Not now, I'm on the phone!"), protective unavailability ("Not now, I've got a friend over!"), protective belligerence ("Not now, I'm in a bad mood!") all conspire to give parents the same forbidding message: "Leave me alone!" If parents wait until a "good time" to raise a concern or communicate a need, they will never get their say. During midadolescence, the best time they are often likely to get is a bad time being given a hard time for intruding into the teenager's life with an unwanted discussion.

Using irascibility to keep parents away is a time-honored strategy for avoiding parental communication during midadolescence. Parents need to brave the threat of unpleasantness, insist on civility, and feel free to initiate whatever needs to be discussed.

Sometimes your teenager at this age will refuse to talk with you about what is going on or about what manner of parenting response you need to make. If you are frozen out in this manner, you can tell your teenager that he or she is giving up power in two important ways. Explain it this way: "It is not my job to make you talk with me, but it is my job to let you know the consequences of not talking with me. In the absence of any information from you, I am going to come to my own understandings of what is happening in your life—which may not be true—and I am going to make independent choices about how to treat you—which you may not agree with. So, if you want to inform my understanding and influence my decisions, you might want to consider talking to me about what is really going on. My ignorance is up to you."

ALERT!

If your teenager complains that you don't understand because the world is different from when you were growing up, agree. Then say, "If you truly want me to understand how life is for young people today, then educate me, tell me about it. I want to learn."

The Power of Peers

In midadolescence a peer group can become a second family of the utmost importance. The more separated from, or opposed to, family a teenager grows, the more attached to friends he or she becomes. (Family changes such as divorce and remarriage often increase teenage dependence on peers.) Through shared experience and adventure, through support and sympathy, peers are there for each other. They provide what parents cannot—companionship in quest of worldly experimentation and social independence.

Belonging

Belonging to a peer group, however, comes at a price. To gain and maintain membership in good standing, the teenager must make certain sacrifices.

- A certain amount of individual freedom is given up because conformity is the price of acceptance. "You have to behave like us, believe like us, look like us, like us best, and not do better than us."
- A certain amount of personal honesty is given up. "You have to pretend to enjoy whatever the group decides to do."
- A certain amount of control is given up. "You have to go along with the group to prove you belong."

There is no such thing as a peer group that does not exert peer pressure. However, no group can pressure your teenager into doing anything without his or her permission. Never accept peer pressure as an excuse for doing wrong. A lot of times a teen's readiness to make a bad decision was just a matter of waiting for the right (or wrong) time to come along.

"But you don't understand," your teenager may protest in his defense. "I couldn't say no!" By this statement, your teenager means that if he doesn't conform, he won't belong. At this point, your teenager needs some disciplinary guidance about how to resist peer pressure without having to say an outright "No." He or she needs some strategies for refusing without losing face or social standing.

Resisting Peer Pressure

Tell your teenager to play for delay when he feels pressure to do what he doesn't want to do. The more he can delay, the more time he buys to think his way out of the situation. So he can say, "I don't feel like doing that right now." And if peers get on him for refusing, he can get right back on them. He can get angry: "I didn't say not ever, I said not now. And I don't like being pushed around! Not by anyone!" (They can respect that.)

Or he may propose doing something else first. "I'm hungry. I want to get something to eat before we do that." That's another way to play for delay. Or he can say he needs to use the bathroom, taking time alone to gather time to think. Yet another delay.

Delay often works because group ideas tend to be ruled by impulse, so that what everyone was thinking of doing before he went to the bathroom may have changed direction by the time he comes out. Finally, you can also give him permission to use you for a lie. "I'd like to try some of that stuff, but it's not worth it. My parents test me for drugs, and if I ever show up positive, they'll put off my ever driving a car."

Finally, not all peer pressure leads young people astray by compelling them to act together in ways each would not act alone. It can also offer protection. Friends do look out for friends, often keeping them out of trouble. Not all peer pressure is bad. When your teenager states, "We take care of each other," he or she is often telling the truth.

 **QUESTION?**

Why do teenagers have so much trouble saying no to peers when saying no to parents is so easy?
Because refusal won't drive away parental love, but it may well jeopardize standing with peers.

Adolescent Lies

When your son or daughter enters midadolescence and begins pushing harder for freedom to grow, you may begin to wonder, "Whatever happened to the truth?" He or she seems more prone to lie both by commission (telling a deliberate falsehood) and by omission (not voluntarily disclosing all that parents need to know).

Insisting on the importance of truth, you may want to declare where you stand on this subject. "In the course of growing up, I expect you to try some things I wish you wouldn't. However, if you hide them from me, or if you lie to my face, I will feel hurt and angry. Being told the truth about what you do is more important to me than agreeing with all you do. I intend to hold both of us to honest account with each other so you keep me adequately informed about your actions and I keep you adequately informed about my opinions in response."

The Risks in Lying

In general, adolescents tend to lie more than children. Why? Lies are usually told for freedom's sake. For many teenagers, particularly during midadolescence when freedom feels so important, lying seems to be the easy way out of trouble or into adventure that has been disallowed. But lying is deceptive: What seems simpler at the moment becomes complicated over time. The "easy way out" turns out to be extremely expensive, particularly for teenagers who have gotten so deep into lying that they have a hard time getting out.

For these young people, it can be helpful for parents to itemize the high cost of lying in order to encourage a return to truth. What to tell the errant teenager? Explain some of the common costs of lying.

- **Liars injure other people's feelings with the lies they tell.** Parents who are lied to can feel hurt because lies take advantage of their trust, can feel angry because of being deliberately misled, and can feel frightened because now they don't know what to believe.
- **Liars are punished twice.** If the teenager is found out, he or she is punished twice—first for the offense and second for lying about it.
- **Liars have to lead double lives.** Liars have to remember what they really did (the truth of what happened) and the lie they told about what they did (the falsehood they created). Because they have two versions of reality to manage, not one, telling lies proves twice as complicated as telling the truth.
- **Liars live in fear of discovery.** Concealing the truth, liars have to live in hiding. They start acting fugitively in the family, living in some degree of fear of being found out.
- **Liars become confused by all the lies they tell.** Covering up one lie with another, pretty soon liars lose track of all the lies they've told and find it harder and harder to keep their story straight.
- **Liars lower their opinion of themselves.** Because they lack the courage to own up to the truth of their actions, liars live a coward's life; each time they run from the truth, they run their self-esteem further down.
- **Liars become isolated.** To stay away from questions and to keep from being found out, liars distance themselves from family, increasingly cutting off open communication with those they love.

- **Liars believe their own lies.** What begins as lying to others ends up as lying to themselves as liars lose track of what really happened and come to believe some of the untruths they have told.
- **Liars feel hurt from hurting others.** Having abused and exploited the trust of those they love, liars end up feeling guilty for the damage they have caused.
- **Liars "make" people angry.** Each time they are found out, liars must deal with people who resent being manipulated by lies.
- **Liars lose credibility.** The more lies are told and found out, the harder it becomes for people to believe liars when they are actually telling the truth.
- **Liars arouse suspicion.** People who have been lied to about one thing begin to wonder if they've been lied to about other things as well.
- **Liars lose intimacy.** With each lie they tell, estrangement builds in their relationships because intimacy depends on honesty.
- **Liars are usually relieved when they're found out.** Even though they may have to pay their dues for lying by accepting punishment, liars feel better to be out from under all the pressures that dishonesty created.
- **Liars victimize themselves.** Although lied-to people feel mistreated, because of all the costs they pay, liars mistreat themselves most of all.
- **Liars learn the lesson of lying.** Liars learn that it is far easier to be the person lied to than to be the one who has been telling all the lies.

Given so many costs of lying, why do children, and particularly teenagers in midadolescence, lie? Lying is generally done in order to gain illicit freedom, conceal a harmful truth, create a false impression, or avoid getting into trouble.

Teaching Your Teen Not to Lie

Parents need to treat lying seriously. The quality of family life depends on the quality of communication, and lying can erode that quality to devastating effect. There is no trust without truth. There is no intimacy without honesty. There is no safety without sincerity. And there is no such thing as a small lie, because when parents overlook one lie, they only encourage the telling of another.

ALERT!

> Tell your lying adolescent: There are many compromises to be made in healthy relationships, but compromising about truth is not one of them. Without honesty, there can be no trust.

So, when your teenager lies, what can you do to help?

- Explain the high costs of lying so the child understands the risks that go with dishonesty.
- Declare how it feels to be lied to so the child understands how loving relationships can be emotionally affected by dishonesty.
- Apply some symbolic reparation for the lie—a task the child must do that he or she would not ordinarily have to do, to work off the offense.
- When your child has told a lie to someone outside of the family, close the loop of responsibility by making the child get back to the person lied to with a corrected version of the truth.
- Offer the child who impulsively or automatically lies a second chance to rethink the lie just told and correct it with the truth, no penalty attached.
- Insist on a full discussion about why the teenager lied, what steps will be taken by the teenager to prevent further lying, and what the teenager may need from the parents in order to make future truth-telling easier to do.

- Declare that lying in the family will always be treated as a serious offense.
- Finally, declare that you intend to reinstate trust and the expectation of truth in order to give the child a chance to resume an honest footing with you, and so you do not drive yourselves crazy with distrust.

Keep the Trust

To some parents, this last piece of advice will seem wrong. "Shouldn't my child have to wait to earn back my trust after having lied to me?" No. In a healthy family, people trust each other to tell the truth. It is healthy for a parent to trust a child. It is healthy for a child to be trusted. It is healthy for that child to honor trust with truth.

So, when a child lies, treat that dishonesty as a major rule violation by applying some symbolic consequence (some task to be worked off) and then let the child know that hereafter you will trust in being told the truth. If your child keeps lying, you keep dealing with each incident as a major rule violation, applying some consequence, and afterward you keep reinstating trust. The message is, "In a healthy family, people can expect to trust each other's word, and that is the expectation to which you will be held."

Following these guidelines for discipline, you can get through your teen's midadolescent years with a minimum of pain and a maximum gain. Your child is growing up responsibly, thanks to you.

CHAPTER 19

Late Adolescence (Ages 15–18)

L ATE ADOLESCENCE generally encompasses the high school years. As a new freshman, your teen faces a new world—awed by the size of the institution, intimidated by older and more experienced students, and excited by growth possibilities that did not exist before. Wanting to catch up with what older students are able to do increases the desire for more independence. An enormous amount is taught in high school, but most of it is not from classroom instruction. It is derived indirectly from the experiences of other students and directly by acting more grown up and learning from playing the part.

Late adolescence ends for many young people with a mixture of triumph, loss, anxiety, and regret. There is triumph from knowing that one has actually completed high school. There is loss as one's community of friends begins to disband and disperse. There is anxiety about managing the next step into a larger world or job or further education. And there is regret that the simpler time of living at home and going to school is over, and now the true complexity of finding one's way in the world begins.

Most discipline problems in late adolescence are "speed violations" from wanting to grow up too fast. So the parents' job is tricky: You want to support more grown-up behaviors but at a "reasonably" slow pace, governed by judgment and responsibility, not driven by pressure and impulse.

The Learning Curve of High School

Late adolescence is all about learning to act more grown up. How does the teenager learn in high school? From direct experimentation with new and different experiences and from vicarious learning about the exploits of others. The more your freshman teenager (through looking older or through acceleration based on academic, athletic, or other ability) is thrown into the company of juniors and seniors, the steeper and swifter this learning curve becomes.

Finding a Place

Therefore, during freshman year in high school, support ways that your child can associate socially with same-age friends. At the same time, so that he or she can get a social foothold, insist that your teenager join some extracurricular group that first year. Being on an entry-class athletic team or being in band, for example, can immediately provide a group to which he or she can belong. The more disconnected and lonely an entering student is, the more likely it is that he or she will be befriended by students already on the social fringe with adjustment problems of their own.

 **ESSENTIAL**

To catch hold during the first year in high school, freshmen need their parents' supervisory support to help them learn to live within school rules, join an organized student group, and keep up with the more challenging academic work.

There's a lot of pressure to grow up fast when you're at the bottom of the age heap. Being told that you are "only a freshman" is hardly a compliment. No wonder growing up fast, by gathering knowledge and experience, is what many freshmen try to do. No wonder senior year is glamorized as the pinnacle of social power and sophistication. Seniors are supposed to know it all because they have experienced so much, and to have it all because now they "rule the school."

Except, when students do get to senior year, the anticipated glamour is tarnished by the harsh reality. The greatest year in high school usually does not live up to its reviews. Now the teen must deal with letting go—of childhood friends, of high school, of home. He or she may never live in such a large community of friends again. And it will be many years before he or she is able to create an independent sense of home and family to rival the one being left behind.

 **ALERT!**

> Do not turn a teenager's bedroom to another use when he or she has moved out into an apartment or off to college, and do not get rid of old belongings left behind. Having a secure and familiar place in the family to return to when want or need arises makes it feel safer to leave.

Gaining Independence

Come high school, three grown-up activities are now within your teenager's reach, each one of which empowers your son or daughter, like a rocket, to be able to act in more adult ways. His or her desire for more independence is dramatically increased, particularly if two or more of these "rockets" fire off at once. Now you have a more headstrong teenager to deal with than you had before.

What are these three rockets to independence, and why are they so powerful?

- Being old enough to drive a car causes the teenager to believe that this independent mobility means "I can come and go as I desire!"
- Being old enough to hold a part-time job causes the teenager to believe that earning independent income means, "If I make my own money, then I can make my own choices!"

- Being old enough to socially date and party causes the teenager to believe that going out means "If I can go out and take someone out, then I can act socially grown up."

Although parents want their teenager to be able to do all three adult activities, they want these new freedoms—because freedoms are what they are—to be kept within responsible bounds. Thus, you let your adolescent know he or she can do none of these activities without your permission, which you will give only so long as he or she is responsibly taking care of business at home, at school, and out in the world. What you don't want is for your teenager to combine all three grown-up freedoms into a lifestyle that takes over the young person's life. Thus, a part-time job pays for a car, a car enables dating, dating is expensive, and so more hours must be spent on the job. Who has time for chores or schoolwork now?

Driving a Car

Ask any teenager—a car is the "freedom machine." No longer dependent on parents to drive them where they want to go, when they want to go, being able to drive gives teens the freedom to "drive" their own lives. For the young person to rein in all that freedom so it is not abused to harmful cost to self or others takes enormous attention, judgment, and responsibility. It takes being reminded that a car is not a toy to have fun with, it is a transportation device for getting around. The best way for parents to consider whether they want their teenager to drive is to evaluate if their son or daughter is mentally and emotionally equipped to manage the worst degree of risk that driving brings.

Is Your Teen Ready?

Parents should ask themselves, "In our judgment, is our teenager sufficiently mature to be entrusted with the freedom to use a potentially deadly weapon?" At worst, they are turning their teenager loose on the world with an instrument of destruction.

If their son or daughter shows signs of only being out for a good time and has a record of acting impulsively, heedless of consequences, parents should not allow this young person behind the wheel of a car. Driving is a privilege, not a right. Just because the teen has reached the legal driving age does not mean parents are now under some social obligation to let their teenager drive. You should decide your teenager's readiness to drive based on how she is handling other aspects of her life. It is your responsibility to make this determination.

ESSENTIAL

Responsible parents do not allow a teenager with a record of irresponsibility, who shows no signs of changing, to drive at any adolescent age.

The Teen's Responsibilities

Now come the arguments, because having this new freedom inspires desire for more. "What difference can two hours make, whether I'm in at midnight or at two? Nothing can happen to me at two that can't happen to me at twelve." Yes it can. Consider the risk of accidents. The later your teenager stays out, the more likely he or she will encounter a drunk driver, or someone sleepy or asleep at the wheel on the road. The later people stay up and stay out, the more substance use and fatigue are likely to affect choices they make. Your teenager's driving curfew is up to you.

Continuing to allow your teenager to drive depends on his safe driving record. Any moving or other violations will cause you to reevaluate. And any costs arising from such violations will be your teenager's to pay.

In general, having your teenager invest money he's earned to support some of the monthly financing payment (if you've bought him a car), insurance, maintenance, inspection fee, license fees, and gas that are all required for operating a car is helpful.

Assuming part of these responsibilities can cause the teenager to appreciate how expensive this freedom is, and to drive carefully so more expenses from irresponsible driving are not incurred.

Holding a Part-Time Job

Entering the workforce feels like an adult thing to do, and it is. Exchanging labor for money is what your child will be doing throughout his or her adult life. You want your son or daughter to learn the discipline of being able to secure and sustain employment.

There is much good experience your teen can gain from part-time employment. It takes initiative to find a job opening. It takes assertiveness to interview for a position. It takes responsibility to hold a job. It takes obedience to work for a boss. It takes cooperation to work with coworkers. And it takes patience to work with the public (which is what most entry-level jobs require a teenager to do). It also affirms self-worth to know that one has skills for which the world of work is willing to pay money. All of this is on the plus side of the ledger.

 **FACT**

Becoming a wage earner does not reduce the teenager's need for money to spend; it increases it. As income rises, so does the desire to do and have more things that he or she now wants to buy.

On the negative side of the ledger can be investing time at the job at the expense of education, because now making money feels more rewarding than making grades. Also negative can be what is learned from workplace associations—more access to substance use and other unwelcome worldly influences than existed before. Jobs can help teenagers grow up in a hurry as they work alongside older employees.

So parents must see part-time jobs for what they are—an opportunity for growth experience and possibly for harmful exposure. Their job is to monitor the mix so the good outweighs the bad. Since for many teenagers, a cashed paycheck lasts about as long as a lit match, parents may also want to encourage the habit of saving—banking some part of the salary now for spending needs and wants later on.

The Teen Social Scene

Late adolescence is the time when dating becomes more common and partying becomes the socially grown-up thing to do.

Group Socials

In general, dating at first can create discomfort. Most teenagers feel awkward, anxious, even embarrassed about how to act and what to say. Going out with a group is usually more comfortable, and less pressured, than going out with a single person. In addition, casual dating involves less pressure than serious dating. Casual dating tends to focus on fun without loss of freedom from significant involvement. Serious dating tends to focus on enjoying a single relationship and coming to know another person deeply and well.

When serious dating becomes exclusive dating, it can tie a teenager down and may be conducted at the expense of social time with other friends. Now the serious couple must manage tensions around mixing togetherness and separateness, and if infatuation develops, they must also manage tensions from possessiveness and jealousy. Loss of social freedom, distrust of commitment, and fear of betrayal can create discomfort when teenagers fall in love. For teens, being in love usually means being unhappy a lot of the time.

Teen Couples

In general, parents want to encourage low-pressure socializing—group and casual dating, keeping sufficient social freedom to have recreation time for other friends. If your teen gets seriously attached to someone, however, make sure you get to know your teenager's girlfriend or boyfriend. That will maximize your chance to influence the conduct of that relationship. If you oppose the relationship on principle that they are "too young" to be serious, you risk driving them even closer together in response to your opposition.

On whatever level it occurs, however, you need to give your teenager your expectations for keeping dating respectful. Here are four questions for you to ask your teenager about the relationship—he or she should be able to answer yes to all of these to keep it respectful.

- **"Do you like how you treat yourself in the relationship?"** For example, he may like the freedom he gives himself to speak up, to say what he wants to say, to be honestly and authentically himself without any need for pretense.
- **"Do you like how you treat the other person in the relationship?"** For example, she is open to hearing what the other person has to say, she's honest in response, and she can listen when the two disagree without criticizing or correcting the other person's point of view.
- **"Do you like how you are treated in the relationship?"** For example, he may like how in conflict with the other person, she never threatens or demeans him, and he appreciates never feeling pressured to do anything he doesn't want.
- **"Does the other person like how you treat him or her in the relationship?"** For example, the other person may like how she is willing to listen, to compromise on decisions, and doesn't always have to get her way.

 **ALERT!**

Tell your teenager, "How you treat other people is one measure of how you treat yourself. If you mistreat others, then you are treating yourself as someone who treats people badly. If you are respectful of other people, then you are treating yourself as someone who treats people well."

Parties

Parties can be a problem for teenagers (and many adults) because teens lack the social confidence and communication skills to meet and greet and chat with people they may or may not know. That's where the "get-to-know-you drug"—alcohol—comes in, providing the liquid courage to loosen up and feel less self-conscious about how one looks and what one says. Smoking cigarettes gives nervous hands something to do. Partying for the sake of partying can be very hard for many teenagers (and many adults) to do without the support of substances, particularly alcohol and cigarettes.

Attending a social get-together built around an activity or an event reduces the need for substance use. Now there is a planned focus for what everyone is there to do in order to have fun. Having social activities that have a purpose reduces social discomfort because it makes clear how everyone is to act. When you are hosting a party for your teenager, have plenty of activities available (and snacks for them to eat), in addition to announcing that it must be a substance-free occasion. This also means controlling the guest list, keeping a discreet but observable presence, and not allowing any crashers. If you want to know how to design a substance-free social get-together for teenagers, check with youth leaders at area churches. They do it successfully all the time.

ALERT!

Leave a social teenager alone in charge of your home or apartment when you're away overnight and you may risk hosting an "empty house party." All it takes is having a few friends over, others arriving uninvited, and soon the "fun" grows into trouble and out of your teenager's control.

The Culture of Sex

In late adolescence, the pressures to have a complete sexual experience become more intense. Sex is used as a popular topic in entertainment and to sell a universal range of products. If advertisers can somehow find a way to make a product sexy, or associate it with a sexual image, it stands a better chance of enticing consumer interest, while sexual content is standard fare in shows, in print, and in songs. The media is filled with male and female sexual images illustrating or implying the power and pleasure of sexy appearance and sexual behavior.

Given this constant commercial assault since early childhood, how could adolescents not be preoccupied with sex as they grow up? Even more influential than the sexual images presented are the sexual roles that impressionable adolescents are groomed to play. Believe the images, and women are primarily supposed to be sexual attractors, trained to be preoccupied with their appearance to win male attention. Believe the images, and men are primarily supposed to be sexual aggressors, coached to act manly to win female admiration.

To see these images in action, just attend any high school football game where young women in form-fitting costumes cheer and dance, and young men bulk up in pads to show how hard they can play a collision sport. No wonder so many teenagers believe that emulating these images and acting out these roles are how they are meant to excite interest from the other sex.

 **FACT**

> The American Psychological Association reported in 2002 that about half of all high school students, when surveyed, admitted to having had sexual intercourse.

So what are you, as a parent, supposed to do to help your teenager grow beyond the restrictive sexual stereotypes the culture sends? Send more humanizing messages of your own. Let your daughter know that her value as a person is not limited to how beautiful she looks, and let your son know that his value as a person is not limited to how toughly he competes. And when it comes to socializing with the other sex, recommend that they aim for friendship first. Good friends tend not to get good friends into trouble sexually.

Sexual Gaming

Growing up primarily in same-gender peer groups through elementary school and into middle school, girls tend to rely on each other for emotional support, sharing experiences and talking together, confiding to create intimacy. Girls are often socialized to base their self-esteem on their relationships. Boys tend to rely on each other for competition, sharing adventures and risk taking together, testing themselves against each other to create companionship. Boys are often socialized to base their self-esteem on their performance.

By late adolescence, when there is more social and cultural pressure for sexual mixing, males and females can approach each other with very different motivations. A teenage girl may treat a boy as a relationship challenge, as a chance for social completeness—to get a boyfriend. A teenage boy may treat a girl as a performance challenge, as a chance for sexual conquest— to get a girl.

Now begins the gaming to "get" each other in different ways. Some of the common stereotypes each has about the other at this age tell more of the story. For boys, girls are "all teases, out to tie you down." For girls, boys are "all hormones, always on the make."

"True love" does not strike most teenagers in late adolescence, because of all the social gaming that gets in the way. Although sexual pressure is not all one-sided, it is more often aggressive male insistence that wears female resistance down. Sometimes a bad sexual bargain can be made. Insists the boy, "If you really loved me, you'd sleep with me," offering the lure of commitment in exchange for sex. Sometimes a girl feels something is wrong with her if she refuses. Insists the boy, "What's the matter, don't you care?"

Sometimes a boy, instead of taking no for an answer, treats it as a challenge to overcome, relentlessly keeping after a girl who, in his view, is playing hard to get. At last, the girl may give in just to get the pressure over. Then the word gets out. Boasting about his conquest, how he has "scored," the boy gets labeled as a "stud," while the girl is scorned as loose or easy and is called a "slut." Of course, this sexual double standard that tarnishes a girl's reputation and burnishes a boy's is a lie. It takes two to make a stud, and it takes two to make a slut.

 **FACT**

The more sexually exploitive a teenager acts, and the more he or she is sexually exploited by others, the more difficulty he or she will have establishing and maintaining a committed, loving intimacy later on in life.

Given the sexual gaming that goes on in high school, parents need to encourage their late adolescents to be careful how they play. Tell your teenager gaming for sex just ends with someone, usually the girl, getting hurt. Tell your son you don't want him pressuring, manipulating, or exploiting girls for sexual conquest. You don't want aggression used for sexual ends because that can lead to rape, forcing sex on a girl. (Date rape is the most common rape of all.) And you don't want sex used for aggressive ends because that can lead to sexual assault, using sex as a means to inflict physical harm.

Tell your daughter you don't want her to let herself be sexually exploited.

- "If you keep setting sexual limits and the boy keeps testing them, then he is not respecting your limits, is not to be trusted, and you should get away."
- "If you have set your sexual limits and he urges you to drink to change how you think, then he is not respecting your sexual limits and you should get away."

- "If you have set your sexual limits and he tries to argue or manipulate you out of them, using emotional extortion to get his way, then he is not respecting your limits and you should get away."

Part of a parent's disciplinary job during their teenager's high school years is teaching their son or daughter how *not* to play the sexual gaming game.

Romantic Relationships

Although starting a relationship with sex rarely leads teenagers into love, falling in love can often lead them into having sex as a physical affirmation and culmination of the emotional attachment they feel. One level of intimacy naturally leads to another, as all the love stories in all the movies they have ever seen has taught them to believe.

 **ALERT!**

> Take the breakup of a teenage love relationship very seriously. Don't let a rejected boy turn hurt from rejection into anger and try to retaliate. And make sure a rejected girl does not slip from grief into self-destructive despondency from loss. And vice versa!

If your teenager is in a love relationship, he or she is much more likely to have sex. Therefore, if you see love blooming in your teenager's life, you definitely need to talk with him or her about what you wish for this relationship (that it be mutually respectful) and about what you don't wish for this relationship (that it become sexually active). Besides the ordinary dangers of pregnancy and sexually transmitted disease, sexual activity between teenagers often brings them closer than their emotional intimacy can reach, and sex ends up frustrating, straining, and finally estranging the couple.

Having sex only causes them to feel how emotionally far apart they really are. The best advice you can give them is to wait before having sex—wait and give themselves time to emotionally grow together, time to nourish their emotional attachment before they complicate it with sexual loving.

Sex as a Rite of Passage

Most first teenage sex has nothing to do with love. It has to do with seeing sexual intercourse as an important rite of passage into adult life. Those who have had sex often urge their virgin peers along. "Oh, come on, you haven't done it yet? What's the matter with you? When are you going to grow up?!" Although this may sound strange to parents, many teenagers just have sex to get "it" over with. Now the boy can feel like he's a "man." Now the girl can feel like she's a "woman." No wonder so many teenagers need alcohol or drugs to get themselves through an experience they feel they have to have, but do not really want.

So parents may want to give several countermessages.

- "Having sex doesn't make you an adult; being able to make sound and responsible decisions makes you an adult."
- "What you decide to do with your body should depend on what you want and believe, and not on the urgings and opinions of friends."
- "As far as we're concerned, it's more grown up to wait for doing grown-up things like having sex than doing them before you're ready and risking harm."

What to Say about Having Sex

Responsible parents recommend sexual abstinence to their teenagers. Abstinence doesn't mean "not ever"; it means "not yet." It means delay, because the later an adolescent can wait to begin, the more judgment from maturity will govern decision-making and the less likely it is that harm will follow. It is worth advising teenagers that substance intoxication and sexual arousal are both mood- and mind-altering experiences—what seems wise is often not as compelling as what feels good. In both cases, impulse is encouraged, or allowed to take charge. When the two are combined, your teenager is much more likely to try sexual intercourse. Tell your teenager that the best way to prevent unwanted or problem sex is by staying sober.

But suppose your teenager tells you that sometime this year, he or she is probably going to have sex. You're running a home, not a jail. You can inform choice, you can't control it. You can't tie your teenager down or lock the young person up. Repeat why you do not believe it is in his or her best interests to have sex at this early age: It can confuse feelings, hurt self-image, complicate relationships, affect reputation, cause pregnancy, create parental responsibility, transmit sexual disease, and even result in death. It may also be against your moral values or religious faith.

 **ESSENTIAL**

The most powerful preventions against premature sexual involvement in late-adolescent dating are true friendship for each other and maintaining chemical sobriety when together.

Then, give some guidelines for safely doing that which you do not want the teenager to do. "If you are determined to have sex, then have a plan so it is intentional and not accidental. Be sober and do it with a person you trust. Do not feel emotionally or physically forced or trapped. Be responsible and use protection. Do not feel exploitive or exploited. Do not assume that sex means love or love forever, and don't assume that love obligates you to have sex. Don't have sex unless you know that if the relationship ended, you would still feel good about yourself for having had sex. And do not feel that because you had sex once you are now bound to do it with this person or any other again."

Preparing for Independence

Once your child enters late adolescence (roughly coinciding with the entry into high school), you need to be thinking ahead to when high school is over. What happens then? Often the next step is going off to college or getting a job—in either case, probably moving out of the parents' home into shared living space with one or more roommates. This step will require more separation, freedom, independence, and responsibility than your teenager has known before.

Parents should try to encourage increased responsibility during the high school years so that the next step after high school feels as small as possible. New responsibilities will help the young person feel more prepared to function on his or her own. But how do parents teach this preparation? By teaching exit responsibilities and turning more responsibility over to their son or daughter during the high school years.

Teaching Exit Responsibilities

At age fourteen or fifteen, or when your child starts high school, begin planning for graduation. By graduation, you want your teenager to be empowered with sufficient knowledge about responsible behavior and sufficient experience with taking responsibility to be willing and able to master the next step into more independent living. So freshman year in high school is the time for you to start thinking ahead.

 **FACT**

The more exit responsibilities your teenager has mastered by the end of high school, the smaller and easier the next step into more independence will be.

Begin your teen's freshman year by asking yourself, "What exit responsibilities need to be in place at graduation to empower a successful transition into independence?" If you wait until senior year to ask these questions, you have waited too long. By then, with all the anxieties, distractions, and excitement that often accompany the final year in high school, a crash course in responsibility will not be well received by your teenager. Conflict, not learning, will result.

So, freshman year, list out the basic categories of responsibility in which your teenager will need competency to support more independence. The list is enormous. Then ask yourself the question, "As the parent, at what point along the way through high school, and by what means, do I want to start teaching my teenager each of these responsibilities?"

From these objectives, you can back up and specify a rough sequence and schedule of preparation for teaching your child the significant responsibilities he or she will need to support more independence upon graduation from high school. For example, at what age do you want your child to start to manage a bank account, to balance a checkbook, to use a debit card, to be responsible for budgeting to cover routine expenses, and to save for the unexpected? At what age do you want your child to learn how to do minimum maintenance on a car—changing a flat tire, changing and safely disposing of oil, diagnosing common motor problems? At what age do you want your child learning how to find and hold employment? This list goes on and on.

Turning over More Responsibility

The second part of laying the groundwork for more independence after graduation is turning more responsibility for self-regulation over to your teenager in high school. Consider some of the self-regulatory responsibilities you may want to turn over.

- Being responsible for earning some of his or her personal expense money.
- Managing household needs like food shopping, cooking, cleaning, and laundry.
- Being responsible for budgeting a monthly allowance that covers certain basic living expenses (phone, gas, clothing, lunch, for example).

- Managing homework and school performance.
- Managing basic maintenance of a car (if driving).
- Managing social schedule, curfew, and rest.

These and other responsibilities need to be progressively turned over so that by senior year, you have approximated full freedom of responsibility while your teenager is still at home. That way, should he or she fail in some area, you are still there to help him or her learn from mistakes. (Although these responsibilities are turned over while the teenager is still living at home, your son or daughter still must keep you adequately informed and contribute labor as part of his or her household membership requirements.)

Trial Independence (Ages 18–23)

The last phase of adolescence, trial independence (from after high school through the mid-twenties), is in some ways the most challenging for both young person and parents. A young person faces considerable demands while finding his or her footing as a more independent person in a large and complex world. Living away from home for the first time, getting a job or going to college, sharing living space with a roommate, and being accountable for managing expenses all add up to more social freedom and responsibility than he or she has probably had before.

Parents are often still supplying some support but having less influence over, and more ignorance about, their young person than they had before. "Letting go" may make parents feel helpless and scared. And their fears are not unfounded.

The Risks of Trial Independence

Most young people in trial independence do not find their independent footing right away. Lacking sufficient experience and responsibility, they slip and slide, breaking all kinds of commitments—financial, rental, legal, occupational, educational, and personal, among others—driving down self-esteem in the process.

"What's the matter with me? I'm twenty years old, I keep messing up, and I can't get my life together!"

In addition, they may have no clear direction in life; no job path into the future they want to follow. "I don't know what I want to do!" Anxieties abound in the face of challenges posed by independence. To make matters worse, they are surrounded by a cohort of peers who are mostly feeling and acting the same, often escaping frustration and sense of failure by partying. As this period of maximum alcohol and drug use begins, more dangerous drugs appear.

Lifestyle stress is common at this age. Your college-age child faces:

- Sleep deprivation from late-night living.
- Lack of adequate nutrition from a snack-food diet.
- Debt from overspending.
- Deadline pressure from leaving demands to the last minute.
- Social loneliness when alone and insecurity in groups.
- Aimlessness from lack of goals.
- Alcohol and drug use to self-medicate discomfort and escape cares.
- Lowered self-esteem from feeling developmentally incompetent at an age when competence is expected.

It's no wonder that at this age, some young people are susceptible to despondency, anxiety, exhaustion, and substance abuse.

From Managing to Mentoring

A disciplinary shift is now required of parents if they want to help their son or daughter navigate this final and most challenging period of adolescence. They must give up the management strategies (with the exception of acceptance and affirmation) described so far in this book. They must let go of all corrective discipline. They are no longer in the business of making decisions for the young person or bending the conduct of his or her life to their will.

The disciplinary power that parents can now provide is mentoring, not managing. You can offer counsel and instruction as a mature source of life experience that your young person can freely come to for support, understanding, and advice when the going gets tough.

 **ESSENTIAL**

Do not abandon your adolescent during trial independence. He's outgrown your corrective discipline, but he still needs your instruction. He needs you as a mentor.

As mentors, you should not tell your young person what to do or "make" him or her do anything. You should no longer bail your child out of difficulty. You should not express disappointment, criticism, frustration, anger, worry, or despair. Instead, listen empathetically, advise if asked, let go of any responsibility for fixing whatever is going wrong, and offer faith that your young person, having chosen his or her way into trouble, has what it takes to choose his or her way out. You are nonevaluative, noninterfering, respectful, constant, and loving.

If your young person, having failed to find independent footing out in the larger world, needs to come back home for a short while to stay, support this decision on a mutually agreed upon, limited-time basis. You should agree to this return so that your son or daughter can have a safe place and a simplified time to rethink, recover, and then re-enter the world to try independence again.

As mentors, experienced with your own trial-and-error education in life, you help the young person sort out what went well, what went awry, and what might work better next time. Let your son or daughter know that mistakes are one foundation for learning, and the only real failure in life is the failure to keep on trying.

CHAPTER 20

Constructive Conflict

DISAGREEMENT BETWEEN parent and teenager is one defining feature of adolescence. Yet, an increase in conflicts does not necessarily mean that parent and teenager don't along. More conflict is *how* they get along. The teenager fights for freedom and the parent fights for responsibility.

Although you had disagreements over discipline with your child, come his or her adolescence (around ages nine to thirteen), your child will find even more opportunities for conflict. Your teenager is willing to fight for more independence, the right to individuality, and the need for less parental restraint. These become recurrent issues you argue about. He now complains about how your disciplinary stands get in the way of his freedom to grow.

No matter how little household help you require, you will be told you are demanding too much. No matter how much oversight you let go, you will be told you are overprotective. No matter how much you try to listen, you will be told you don't understand. No matter how much you explain them, you will be told your rules don't make sense. No matter how much you allow and provide, you will be told that friends are allowed and provided more. No matter how just you try to be, you will be told you are unfair. No matter how informed and up to date you try to be, you will be told that you are hopelessly out of touch with reality and behind the times. Come your child's adolescence, it often seems in his or her eyes that a "bad" parent is the best parent you can be.

Your willingness to constructively and respectfully engage in conflict over disciplinary issues for the sake of your teenager's best interests—against what he or she may want—is a major part of your parental responsibility during adolescence.

 **FACT**

Having some differences is unavoidable, and experiencing some conflict is inevitable, but violence is neither. It is up to parents to teach and monitor safety in the conduct of family conflict.

Why Conflict Is Necessary

Conflict is the process of communication through which family members confront and resolve inevitable differences in wants, values, beliefs, perceptions, and goals that arise between them. Because adolescence is the time when your child begins to differentiate herself from the child she once was, from how you are as parents, and from how you want her to be, there are many more differences for parents to deal with during their daughter's teenage years.

Consider how the potential for conflict is built into family life. There may be conflict over cooperation: Who shares what? There may be conflict over control: Whose way shall prevail? There may be conflict over competition: Who gets most? There may be conflict over conformity: Who goes along with whom?

These kinds of conflicts give rise to common grievances from adolescents.

- **Cooperation:** "Why do I need to help?"
- **Control:** "Why can't I decide for myself?"
- **Competition:** "Why don't we ever do what I want?"
- **Conformity:** "Why do I have to do what the family does?"

The Nature of Conflict

Conflict is not fundamentally about disagreement. It is about agreement—two parties agreeing to actively disagree and contest a difference between them. When parent and teenager both agree to disagree over chores, curfew, or cleaning up, and to resolve that difference through argument, then conflict occurs. Conflict is always a matter of mutual choice.

Cooperating in Conflict

Put another way, conflict is always cooperative. It takes two to create a fight. As the bumper sticker asks, "Suppose they gave a war and nobody came?" Or only one party came? There would be no war. So one formula for conflict is:

CONFLICT = RESISTANCE VERSUS RESISTANCE

This is a helpful formula to remember when your teenager, after a bad day at school, is looking for an argument, but you are not. "You never let me do anything!" your teenager begins, inviting you into disagreement. But you choose not to argue in response, so no argument takes place. Instead you offer a different option: "If you've had a hard day, I'd be willing to hear about it." By refusing to resist back, you set limits on how much conflict you are willing to cooperate in. By responding to the underlying feeling, you are being empathetic and offering to listen.

Although you may feel you should fight for what is right every time, you cannot emotionally afford to fight about every difference that arises between you and your teenager. One secret of parent survival in adolescence is being careful to choose your battles wisely.

Picking Your Battles

For most parents, conflict with their teenager is stressful. It feels frustrating, and frustration can cause anger. Sometimes discomfort with one's own or the other person's anger causes anxiety. In either case, it has a negative effect on your attitude. In addition, conflict with their teenager can be contagious when, after arguing with their adolescent, parents find themselves bickering with each other.

 **FACT**

> The most powerful influence on how children engage in conflict is how their parents conduct conflict, so model the approach you want. Your kids learn from watching how you disagree with each other and with them.

For most teenagers, however, conflict with parents is not a source of stress. It is just fighting for freedom as usual. It even has some positive aspects to it. It can be a chance to express built-up bad feelings, to test power by challenging authority, and to assert individuality by taking stands for independence. In most cases, the contest is a mismatch, like out-of-shape amateurs (the parents) exchanging blows with a well-conditioned professional (the teenager). So after one of these rounds is over, while parents have a need to lie down and recover from the exertion, their teenager is not even winded, talking on the phone to a friend as if nothing particular has happened.

Thus, to conserve energy and moderate stress, parents need to be selective about which differences between themselves and their teenager they wish to actively oppose. If they do not exercise this selective control, they may end up feeling like "battered parents," cooperating in more conflict than is good for them. Parents must remember that conflict with their teenager is always a matter of choice.

The Dance of Conflict

Sometimes, parents will object to the notion that they have a role in supporting unwanted conflict with their teenager. Thus, a single-parent father will describe a ritual conflict that unfolds five days a week with his adolescent daughter, who he truly believes is responsible for the end-of-day fighting between them. "As soon as she walks in from school, she starts it," he declares. "She won't do as I ask. She won't begin her chores. It's all her fault." But diagramming the interaction tells a somewhat different story.

As soon as she walks in the door, her father asks her to begin her chores. In response, his daughter complains: "I'm tired. I'll do them later!" Now the father stops asking and demands: "I told you to start your chores now!" In response, his daughter argues: "You never give me a chance to unwind after school. I need some time to relax." Now her father, to show he means business, adds on an additional assignment: "For refusing to do your regular chores, you can have some more to do as well!" In response, his daughter refuses: "That's not fair! There's no way I'll do extra!" Now her father threatens: "If you don't do as you're told, there'll be no going out this weekend!" Now his daughter explodes: "You always punish me when you don't get what you want!" Now her father explodes: "You never do what you're asked!" The fight, which has by now become a ritual of daily life during the week, commences, father and daughter trading angry accusations back and forth to no good effect.

 **ALERT!**

> Parents who blame their teenager for fighting with them all the time are not taking their share of responsibility for the conflict. If they want to reduce the fighting, then they need to cooperate in conflict less.

This conflict is so well practiced that it takes less than a minute to fully develop. Then, when both parties run out of angry energy and separate to get relief, the daughter does what she was initially asked. Asked why she went through all that conflict only to end up complying with her father's initial request, she replies, "Because I don't like being pushed around when I get home. He doesn't have to always greet me with a chore right away. He does have different choices, you know!" And she's correct. They both could make different choices. He could choose not to immediately ask, demand, add on, and threaten. She can choose not to immediately complain, argue, and refuse. But this sequence has become so automatic on both sides, that each feels trapped by the other, totally blames the other, feels helpless and a victim, and so has no way out.

The way to stop the conflict is not for them to change each other, but to take individual responsibility for the cooperative choices each of them is making. By changing those choices, they can keep the conflict from happening. So, the father might make some changes in his choices. "When you come home, the first thing I want is to hear how your day was. The second is to give you time to unwind. And the third is to get some help around the house." The daughter could also make some changes in her choices. "When I come home, the first thing I want you to know is that I don't want you to do all the family work yourself. The second is I want a couple of minutes to catch my breath. And the third is I want to start giving you the help I know you need." So now they start to work with each other and not against each other.

Communication in Conflict

Conflict is not something you have with your teenager. It is something you *do* with your teenager. It is an act of performance. Every time you agree to cooperate in conflict with your teenager, you provide one more training experience in how to conduct conflict that your teenager will carry into future relationships. How your teenager learns to handle conflict with you now is how he or she will likely handle conflict in significant relationships later in life.

In any conflict between you, the issue that you are differing over is actually the second priority. Because frustration with opposition can lead to anger that can cause family members to speak or act in ways they later regret, the first priority in family conflict is always managing emotional intensity. When in conflict with your teenager, you each need to take responsibility for monitoring your respective emotional states so your actions and words do not become destructive. If either of you finds yourself heating up, then declare a timeout, take a break, separate, cool down, then re-engage in a more emotionally sober and rational way.

 **FACT**

> In family conflict, the number one priority is keeping the process of communication safe for all involved. Letting the argument get heated can result in destructive words or actions that damage relationships.

Here is a riddle to keep in mind: "What do humans and most other animals have in common when in conflict?" The answer is, "They all fight with their mouths." For people, this means minding their use of words because words can "bite." That old maxim, "Sticks and stones can break my bones but words can never hurt me," is simply untrue. In family conflict, words do most of the damage. Thoughtless, impulsive, or angry words can inflict wounds that are slow to heal because they are difficult to forget. Your primary job in conflict with your teenager is to model and monitor the use of language, keeping it constructive and respectful, teaching your adolescent to do the same.

Tactics to Avoid

There are two kinds of tactics that teenagers commonly use in conflict that parents must refuse to play along with and must not use themselves: distraction and manipulation. Both tactics undermine the conflict resolution process by getting in the way of honest, open, and direct communication about the issue at hand. Distraction tactics are used to keep from losing. Manipulation tactics are used to "force" a win.

Distraction Tactics

The adolescent resorts to distraction tactics in arguments that he or she is losing, trying to change the focus to an issue where there is a better chance of winning. Suppose you want to discuss with your twelve-year-old son why he's not turning in his homework, and what needs to change to solve this. You start by dealing with the specific: "You have not been turning in your homework this week." Rather than reply to the specific issue for which he has no defense, he tries to shift the topic to an abstract complaint: "The only thing you care about is how I do in school!"

But you stick to the issue, restating it with accuracy: "Your teacher told me that the last four days, you have not turned in your homework." Having no accurate data to counter this charge, he now resorts to using extremes: "You never believe me, you always believe the teacher!" But you stick to the issue, restating it in the present: "As matters now stand, you are not turning in your homework." Having no present data to contradict you, he now tries to shift the focus to past and future: "This is just what you do, holding what's already happened against me, refusing to trust that I'll do better next time!"

 **ESSENTIAL**

Do not let your adolescent's distraction tactics cause you to get off the disciplinary point you are determined to resolve.

But you stick to the issue, restating it in terms of responsibility: "It is your job to do your homework and turn it in." Having no evidence of responsibility to refute you, he tries to shift the focus with blame: "It's the teacher's fault for not making sure I wrote the homework down!" But you stick to the issue by sticking to the evidence: "You have not been turning in your homework, and it needs to be done." Having no evidence to defend with, he resorts to excuses: "Maybe I just forgot; people do forget, you know!"

But you stick to the issue by relentlessly staying on the subject:

"You have not been turning in homework and that needs to be done." Having no facts to dispute your charge, he makes one last attempt to shift the focus by getting you off the subject: "You always get after me about school, but never my sister, because she's your favorite!" But you are steadfast. You will not be distracted: "I want to discuss with you why homework is not being turned in and what you need to do so that it is."

Manipulation Tactics

The teenager resorts to manipulation tactics when he or she wants to overcome a refusal you have made. For example, you have just refused your sixteen-year-old permission to attend a late-night party just outside of town to which some of her friends ("all of them," according to her) have been allowed to go. Unable to persuade you out of your decision with reasonable argument, she turns to emotional manipulation to try to change your mind.

Another name for this manipulation is emotional extortion. Long ago, before acquiring speech, the infant/toddler discovered that strong emotional expression could sometimes change a parental no into a yes.

So, first, your teenager uses an expression of love. "I love you so much, you're the most wonderful parent! You always understand me and what I need!" And feeling flattered in response to this expression of emotion, perhaps you re-evaluate your refusal. But in the end, you still say no.

Now, since love didn't work, your teenager may turn to anger. "You never let me do anything! I'll never forgive you for not letting me go!" And feeling rejected in response to this expression of emotion, perhaps you re-evaluate your refusal. But in the end, you still say no.

Now since anger didn't work, your teenager may turn to suffering. "You've made me so unhappy! I'll never get over this hurt!" And feeling guilty in response to this tearful expression of emotion, perhaps you re-evaluate your refusal. But in the end, you still say no.

Now since suffering didn't work, your teenager may turn to helplessness. "Oh, what's the point? My life is all up to you anyway.

There's nothing I can do!" And feeling pity in response to this expression of emotion, perhaps you re-evaluate your refusal. But in the end, you still say no.

Since helplessness didn't work, your teenager may turn to apathy. "You can decide whatever you want. I don't care what—I don't care about you!" And feeling abandoned in response to this expression of emotion, perhaps you re-evaluate your refusal. But in the end, you still say no.

Now since apathy didn't work, your teenager may turn to threat of injury. "You better watch out! I'll get back at you or maybe I'll hurt even myself!" And feeling scared in response to this expression of emotion, perhaps you re-evaluate your refusal. But in the end, you still say no.

 **ESSENTIAL**

Teach your child to value conflict as a way to safely deepen and strengthen caring relationships in the family. Learning this helps your son or daughter to create intimacy around differences in future relationships.

No teenager will use this full arsenal of emotions on any single occasion to try and overcome parental refusal, but he or she will oftentimes resort to the one that parents have proven vulnerable to in the past. By adolescence, a child has come to know his parents extremely well, and he's willing to use that knowledge to create the effect he wants. Thus, if you can't stand feeling guilty, expect your teen to express suffering as a manipulation. If you can't stand feeling rejection, expect anger. If you can't stand feeling fear, expect threat.

Holding your position in the face of this kind of emotional onslaught is not easy, but it is necessary. Emotions should be used to express authentic feelings, not to manipulate people to get one's way in conflict. You want to keep disagreement declarative so differences can be discussed and rationally resolved. To this end, you refuse to play emotional extortion with your teenager, and you refrain from using it yourself. (For a fuller discussion of these "get my way" techniques, see *Declare Yourself* by John Narciso.)

Rules for Family Conflict

Conflict can be dangerous. In war, the outcome (who wins) is more important than the process (any means necessary) because victory is all that counts. In families, the process (how people communicate) is more important than the outcome (the resolution reached) because protecting the future of the relationship is paramount. Adults who were "attack trained" in fighting growing up are at risk of using wartime tactics in family conflict, to destructive effect.

 **FACT**

> Most acts of family violence and social hate crimes are preceded by namecalling.

In caring relationships, learning to fight well is the work of a lifetime. Being able to confront, discuss, and resolve significant differences without anyone's ever suffering harm takes disciplined conduct. To teach this discipline, it helps to have guidelines and restraints in place to keep conflict constructive. A few such "rules for family conflict" are listed here.

• **Keep conflict safe.** Conflict is never an acceptable excuse for doing another family member harm. "Well, I only said that because I was angry" is no excuse. If anger caused anyone to do or say something hurtful, then another way to manage that anger must be found. Any injury received in family conflict should be accidental, never intentional.

• **Have an injury agreement in place in case conflict ever causes, or threatens to cause, harm.** Whenever, in the course of conflict, anyone feels endangered or actually hurt, the issue at difference should immediately be put aside and the hurtful behavior addressed in such a way that it will not occur again. Then conflict over the difference can safely proceed again.

• **Offer both parties the right of separation and a responsibility for return.** Anytime either party in a conflict is getting too worked up emotionally and feels at risk of saying or doing something he or she might later regret, that person has the right to declare a separation, or a timeout to cool down. At the same time, that person has a responsibility for scheduling a time to return to the discussion when it can be conducted in a more emotionally sober way.

• **Make a commitment not to stop caring.** Particularly for an adolescent, there is a need to know from parents that no matter how hard he or she pushes against authority in conflict, the teenager is in no danger of pushing their love away.

• **Exercise your right and responsibility to speak up.** All parties are entitled to their say, whether others agree with what they say or not, so long as they don't say it in a disrespectful or abusive manner. They are also responsible for speaking up if they want their desire or opinion known. There is no mind reading. Family members can know only what they are told.

• **Agree to discuss the specifics of your differences in specific terms.** Conflicts cannot be resolved by resorting to abstracts and generalizations. Stick to objective descriptions of happenings and events each side wants or does not want to have occur.

• **Avoid meltdowns.** Conflict creates resemblance, with each party tending to copy influential tactics used by the other. Therefore, parents have to model constructive communication so the teenager is encouraged to imitate their conduct and not the reverse. When parents imitate impulsive adolescent behavior in conflict (voice raising, interrupting, and insulting), then a meltdown has occurred—now the parents are communicating on the teenager's terms.

• **Do not allow namecalling.** Namecalling, attaching a negative label to the other person in conflict, is like loading a gun. The bad name can be used to justify bad treatment. "If you're going to act like a crybaby, then I'll really give you something to cry about!"

- **Avoid making extreme statements.** It is easy to trade "You always" and "You never" accusations, both of which distort the other person's record. "On this occasion" is closer to the truth.
- **Do not carry over emotion or issues from one conflict to the next.** There are no carryovers. There is no unfinished grievance left over from a previous conflict to become activated in the next, and there is no anxiety about the next conflict based on how the last one was conducted. Any carryover of either kind needs to be addressed, or your next conflict will be harder to resolve.
- **Remember that the goal in family conflict is intimacy.** There are two ways to get intimacy in relationships—by sharing human similarities and by confronting differences. The goal of conflict is to safely confront differences, talking them through to reach a settlement that both parties can live with, each coming to better know the other and feel better known by the other than was the case before, their relationship strengthened by the understanding and agreement between them.
- **Be empathetic.** Instead of focusing on achieving what you want to get, express concern for what the other person is feeling and needing emotionally. Then discuss your feelings and needs in return, and on the basis of that exchange begin to explore resolution based on mutual understanding of, and empathy for, each other. This is a far more productive way of resolving family conflict than both sides arguing to win their way at the other person's expense.

If you follow these guidelines in conflicts with your teenager, you can handle the inevitable differences between you in nondestructive ways.

Helpful Web Sites

   ✑ *www.OnlyChild.com*
For information on parenting an only child.

   ✑ *www.drugstrategies.com*
For guidance on effective drug treatment programs.

   ✑ *www.carlpickhardt.com*
For monthly articles about parenting by author/psychologist Carl
E. Pickhardt, Ph.D.

   ✑ *www.sfhelp.org*
For information about step relationships from the Stepfamily
Information Program.

   ✑ *www.parentswithoutpartners.org*
For information about single parenting.

   ✑ *www.FamilyEducation.com*
For information about a wide range of parenting

   ✑ *www.parenttrainingcenter.com*
For information about positive discipline.

   ✑ *www.npin.org*
For research-based information about parenting.

✑ *www.parenting-ed.org*

For information about effective parenting.

✑ *www.tnpc.com*

For information from a variety of parenting experts.

✑ *www.thekidsshow.org*

For information about child care, health care, and media impact.

✑ *www.positiveparenting.incaf.com*

For information about redirection as a disciplinary approach.

✑ *www.pocketparent.còm*

For information about positive discipline up to age twelve.

✑ *www.thesuccessfulparent.com*

For information about parenting adolescents.

✑ *www.parents-talk.com*

For information from dialoguing with other parents.

Additional Resources

For Further Reading

Lickona, Thomas, Ph.D. *Raising Good Children* (New York: Bantam Books, 1994).

Lutz, Ericka. *The Complete Idiot's Guide to A Well Behaved Child* (New York: Alpha Books, 1999).

Nelsen, Jane, Ed. D. *Positive Discipline* (New York: Ballantine Books, 1996).

Nelson, Gerald E., M.D. *Good Discipline, Good Kids* (Avon, MA: Adams Media Corporation, 2000).

Pickhardt, Carl, Ph.D. *Keys to Developing Your Child's Self-Esteem* (New York: Barron's, 2000).

Pickhardt, Carl, Ph.D. *Keys to Raising A Drug-free Child* (New York: Barron's, 1999).

Pickhardt, Carl, Ph.D. *Keys to Successful Step-fathering* (New York: Barron's, 1997).

Pickhardt, C. E. *The Case of the Scary Divorce— A Jackson Skye Mystery* (Washington, DC: Magination Press, The American Psychological Association, 1997).

Support Groups

Parents Anonymous
✆ (909) 621-6184
Strengthening families, breaking the cycle of abuse, and helping parents create safe homes for their children.

Tough Love
✆ (215) 348-7090
Providing support and guidance for families in trouble, emphasizing problem solving and children's growing into becoming responsible adults.

Al Anon
✆ (888) 4AL-ANON
Helping families recover from a family member's problem drinking.

Circle of Parents
✆ (312) 663-3520
Providing mutual-support groups in which parents can help each other.

WE HAVE EVERYTHING

FOR PARENTING!

From addressing such serious issues as eating disorders and school violence to learning tolerance for pink and blue hair, *The Everything®*
Tween Book provides sound, professional advice on coping with your child's psychological, social, and emotional needs.

Trade paperback,
$14.95 ($22.95 CAN)
1-58062-870-2, 304 pages

The Everything® Homeschooling Book is the perfect handbook to help you take control of your child's education. From researching state curriculum requirements to homeschooling multiple children, this thorough book provides up-to-date information on the best sources for curriculum guidelines by grade level, techniques for designing lesson plans, and more.

Trade paperback,
$14.95 ($22.95 CAN)
1 58062 868 0, 320 pages

Available wherever books are sold!
To order, call 800-872-5627,
or visit us at *www.everything.com*

Everything® and everything.com® are registered
trademarks of F+W Publications, Inc.

UPCOMING TITLES IN THE
EVERYTHING® PARENT'S GUIDE SERIES!